W9-BHB-073

THE ROAD TO YOU

THE ROAD TO YOU

Callings and How We Fulfill Them

Robert J. Furey, PhD

ALBA·HOUSE NEW·YORK

SOCIETY OF ST. PAUL, 2187 VICTORY BLVD., STATEN ISLAND, NEW YORK 10314

ST PAULS

Library of Congress Cataloging-in-Publication Data

Furey, Robert J.
  The road to you: callings and how we fulfill them / Robert J. Furey.
       p.   cm.
  Includes bibliographical references.
  ISBN 0-8189-0762-2
  i. Vocation. 2. Life.   I. Title.
BL629.F87   1997
  158.6 — dc20   96-40978
                                             CIP

Produced and designed in the United States of America by the
Fathers and Brothers of the Society of St. Paul,
2187 Victory Boulevard, Staten Island, New York 10314,
as part of their communications apostolate.

ISBN: 0-8189-0762-2

Printing Information:

Current Printing - first digit   1   2   3   4   5   6   7   8   9   10

Year of Current Printing - first year shown

1997   1998   1999   2000   2001   2002   2003   2004   2005

DEDICATION

To

Grandpop
&
Hollis

Two people who taught me a great deal
about The Road To You

TABLE OF CONTENTS

INTRODUCTION

Throughout time and across culture people have described life as a journey. According to these metaphors, we are travelers constantly moving, and hopefully growing, through all our days. But if life truly is a journey, then there must be a destination. Without this destination life would be only aimless movement without the purpose and direction inherent in a true journey.

The Road to You is about the road, the traveler, and the destination. The journey begins with a yearning, a calling. As the road passes through dragons and shadows, insight and doubt, the traveler becomes prepared to fulfill his or her vision. The road to you takes you to the place where you can live your calling.

In order to benefit most from this book, you must be, at least, prepared to believe that we have callings in life. If the idea of callings is unclear to you, or if you just need to consider the phenomenon further before you are ready to act on this belief, I suggest you read my book *Called By Name*. In the pages ahead I will not spend a great deal of time defending the existence of callings. As I said, this is a book for those who are already prepared to believe.

Much like your life, this book begins with the calling. You see, it is your calling that guides you along the way on the road to you.

THE ROAD TO YOU

CHAPTER ONE

THE YEARNING

The road to you begins with a yearning. You feel yourself pulled beyond yourself toward a destination that may not be immediately understood. The yearning can start at any time. You may begin to feel it in the commuter train or in class or while lying in bed at night. It may speak to you for the first time while you are recovering from surgery or tending to the garden. It may make its initial breakthrough while you are in church or while you are doing the dishes. It may come to you as you gaze at the sunset or in a dream. The yearning begins in a place where it can reach you.

The yearning is your calling. It is your mission, or set of missions, in life. It may come to you in an instant or it may let itself be known to you in a slow gradual awakening. You may accept it gratefully and graciously or you may fight it and try to bury it deep inside yourself in a place where its voice won't be heard. If you choose to force it out of your life, you are not alone. Many people, I'm afraid, resist their callings. Usually they resist out of fear. They fear that they are being called to do more than they can. This would lead to failure, embarrassment or whatever monster they fear most. Then there's the opposite concern. There are those who dread the thought that the tasks they are called to may be judged insignificant. They rationalize their resistance by saying to themselves, "Why would I be called to this when I am capable of so much more?"

Your calling may be the answer to a prayer or it may be the last thing on earth you want to hear. But even when you are unhappy with your calling, the yearning remains. It asks you to look harder at what it is saying. It guides you to free yourself from your misconceptions and the expectations of others who seek to control your life. Its message is unrelenting. There is a job for you to do in this world and it can only be done by you. If you choose to ignore the yearning, your tasks will never be completed. Your calling may ask you to build, organize, heal, or protect. You may be driven to invent, discover, teach, entertain, or explore. You are urged to go where you are needed.

Where the calling originates is a question each of us must answer. At first, people are prone to answer this using the language with which they are most familiar. Certain scientists say that genes produce unique talents in individuals and that these talents shape one's path in life. Some psychologists talk about an inner self that is responsible for directing us. Other psychologists suggest that the unconscious mind has the power to guide us. Still others say we follow the path that reinforces us the most. Then there are those who believe that we are called by God. By this line of thinking, following your calling means following the will of God.

You will have to discover for yourself the source of your calling. Others may help you in your search but, ultimately, you will have to find the voice that calls you. Just as no one else can describe your calling, no one else can tell you what you will encounter as you get closer to its source.

A warning, however, is in order here. The road to you goes beyond you. You do not create your callings. If your calling is the voice of your genes, it wasn't you who put it there. And even if you were to trace this voice to the deepest layers of your unconscious, you would find that the yearning is not your creation. The voice that calls you is not your voice. The yearning you feel pulls you to be more than you ever have been. It drives you to places you've never been. And it doesn't go away even when it endangers the body and unsettles the mind. Your calling may have little survival value.

If a calling were of your own making, you would have control of it. This is not the case. While you do have the freedom to deny it, you do not have the power to control it. You cannot destroy it. It survives your fear or disappointment. It sustains itself even when it is not wanted.

You can push the yearning far into your unconscious but in order to keep it there you would have to spend large amounts of mental energy forcing it out of your awareness. You see, it requires energy, often a great deal of energy, to deny a calling. If it were freed to be used productively, this energy could lend itself to creativity, work, love, humor, play, fitness, or learning. This energy could contribute to courage, perseverance, and determination. All these magnificent qualities that are fueled by energy in the psyche are compromised when the energy is spent denying one's purpose in life.

No matter how much energy is spent on this denial, however, the job is never done completely. A calling can not be repressed forever. It is simply too strong to be silenced. The most desperate attempts to quiet it will never be completely successful. The yearning refuses to be destroyed. It bides its time and seizes its opportunities. Often its strongest breakthroughs come when you don't have the energy to resist it. These instances include periods of physical illness. Many people hear their callings most clearly while in hospital beds. Another common occasion to feel the yearning is during the course of emotional upheaval. Depression, for instance, is one such form of suffering that drains one's mental energy to the point where the yearning may move boldly to the surface. This is why our present treatments for clinical depression are often ineffective. The majority of these remedies recognize the psychological ramifications of depression, yet fail to comprehend the spiritual aspects. Many of these strategies, including certain anti-depressant regimens, only serve to restore the energy needed to continue repressing material that desperately needs to be released and brought more fully into awareness.

Ironically, people often begin their spiritual healing while in the midst of physical and psychological turmoil. Without the energy needed to drive the yearning from consciousness, we are more likely to face the awakening.

Age can also be a factor here. As aging progresses and energy starts to decline, there is less stamina available to support denial. Consequently, material that was locked away moves closer to the light. This partially explains the wisdom that comes to many people as they age.

While a calling is denied it continues to live. Like the phone that refuses to stop ringing or the knock on the door that won't go away, the yearning sends reminders that even in exile it will not die. These reminders may land in any part of our beings. They may gnaw at the ego and thus produce a lowered self-esteem. They may tug at the will which leads to chronic indecisiveness. Perhaps most common of all, however, is the effect a repressed calling has on the conscience. The conscience is especially sensitive to the pangs of callings denied. The pangs lead to guilt feelings, sometimes guilt feelings so strong that they can virtually incapacitate someone.

This guilt may manifest itself in a variety of forms. It can steal one's love for life and lead to withdrawal from human contact or into aggressive or self-destructive behaviors. Living with guilt can be so unpleasant that people have created a never ending list of compulsions and addictions to distract themselves from it. At the root of these destructive behaviors is a person's unwillingness to accept the life they are being called to.

Working through this guilt can be particularly difficult because the person does not want to look at its cause. It was, of course, this refusal to listen to the yearning that brought on the guilt in the first place. The guilt lifts, then, when the individual consciously decides to look at its cause. This may come as a willful decision or due to the fact that one simply no longer has the energy to keep the truth out of awareness.

If we allow it, our callings produce a yearning that points us in our own very special directions. When you develop an awareness of your calling you find your purpose in life and you begin to understand where you belong. The fish is now in the water. The eagle is in the sky. The deer has arrived in the forest.

Accepting your calling means that there is no longer any reason to waste your energy trying to deny who you really are. This energy can now be spent productively to serve your purpose in life. This surge of energy can be tremendously empowering. A calling brings with it spiritual energy. This is, in fact, the most powerful kind of energy a human being will ever know. When you accept your calling, you inherit this energy. As your spiritual energy unites with your physical and psychological energies, a magnificent force begins. This personal power emerges as these three sources of energy begin to harmonize. As the internal conflict is removed, your energies join and focus. Guilt is transformed into empowerment. The desire to conform is replaced by an urge to emerge as your own person with your own special contribution.

BIO-PSYCHO-SPIRITUAL BEINGS

Human nature might be easier to understand if it could be described with a single set of terms. If the study of human nature could be reduced to one discipline such as biology or psychology or theology there might be less confusion about what we are or what we can be or what we ought to be. But, for better or for worse, we are more complex than this. There are different dimensions to the human condition, each one unique and yet connected with each other. Broadly speaking, we have at least three dimensions — the biological, the psychological, and the spiritual. While all three coexist from the time we are born until our final living moment, they each have their own needs and make their own contributions.

At birth we are primarily biological beings. Our behavior is guided by physical needs. Our personalities are little more than the temperaments we come into the world with. Our focus is on acquiring enough food and sleep to survive. Who we are and what we need are determined by our genes. Psychological factors do play a role during infancy but they do not yet have the same clout in influencing the direction and quality of development. The strongest yearning the infant feels is to satisfy his biological drives.

It isn't long, however, before emotional needs gain a significant voice. Some say the first emotional need is to be loved; others have argued that the initial psychological drive is to find security. Determining which of these surfaces first — or whether or not they are, in fact, distinct — is not really necessary for our present purposes. Suffice it to say that love and safety are two powerful needs that enter our lives quite early. If they are not fulfilled adequately, growth can be arrested until they are provided in ample doses. Unfortunately, this sad state of affairs describes a large portion of people alive today. Unable or unwilling to find and provide love or security, they spend their lives looking for what in a healthier world would be their birthright.

As childhood moves into adolescence other psychological needs exert themselves. Notable is the need to belong to a community that one considers valuable. People need to be appreciated by people we respect. This need has existed throughout time and in all cultures. We are social beings. But there are, of course, people who, sadly, never develop the skills necessary to live happily in a human community. These individuals sooner or later get labeled outcasts, loners, or antisocial personalities. They live without adequate human contact in a world filled with hurt, anger, distrust, and suspicion. Many of these people present themselves as though they are happy to be living this way and that their isolation is completely their own choice. But this is only the posturing of frightened, lonely, and discontented beings. Everyone needs to belong to a community. Those who are unwilling to find accepting tribes live pained lives.

So strong is the need to belong that people will amputate parts of their personalities in order to gain acceptance. If the real me is not good enough to be accepted, then I may be willing to alter myself in whatever way is needed to gain entrance. In other words, I will create a false self. This false self may be nothing like my true self. But I will create this mask and wear it around the clock if it will help me gain entry into a valued group. I will wear the mask until it sticks to my skin if that's what I believe it takes. I may even cling to this facade until I am no longer familiar with my true self. This tragedy happens all too often. The true self gets lost because someone fears the social consequences of being who they really are. They lose themselves behind a persona of who they believe others want them to be.

During adolescence we all do this to some extent. No one wants to feel left out. Besides, the real self is still so new and frail that, at the time, it doesn't seem like much of a sacrifice to put it away for awhile. So we surrender ourselves to peer pressure, gender roles, hero worship, and the expectations of authority figures. If we find a place where we "belong," all is well with the world. If we do not, we feel a void that cannot be adequately described in words. During this time of life, high self-esteem means being accepted; low self-esteem means being stranded outside the circle.

So much of what we deal with psychologically during this first part of life involves fitting in. The need for the group feels so strong that the thought of risking acceptance seems absurd. One of the most popular misconceptions about adolescence is that it is a time of nonconformity. Few notions could be farther from the truth. Adolescence is a time of massive conformity. It is an all-out effort to conform for the sake of belonging. This conforming behavior may not meet parental standards and thus it is considered rebellious by those who seek to control them. In reality, however, adolescents desperately seek for a tribe that will accept them.

As adolescence gives way to adulthood, how we approach our need to belong changes. First, the need is not quite as strong. A confident adult is not as willing to compromise on who he is in order to impress. This person understands that there are times in life when, to preserve your integrity, you must stand alone. Second, a healthy adult does not have a desire to *join* a group as much as he hopes to *contribute* to the group. Belonging is valued but it is not enough. Now there is a need to produce something of value. The question is: what?

Age, it should be emphasized, does not an adult make. Many people well into their later years never connect with the urge to emerge and contribute. Instead, they remain fixated at the belong-at-any-cost stage. Their character becomes dominated by a false self; they close themselves off from any calling that asks them to do something that might not be appropriate in their preferred group. They waste untold amounts of energy keeping their real selves buried within and submit themselves to senseless distractions in order to avoid dealing with the unwanted information. People in this condition may attend vigorously to their physical and psychological states. They may have a personal trainer and self-help books to explain every one of their moods. They depend on people they believe to be experts because they refuse to listen to the wisdom that is calling them. Or they may sit on the couch and let life pass them by altogether. Their spirituality is typically little more than conformity to authority. They tend to accept guidance from those who will help them stay in the herd.

Those willing to emerge and become what only they can become, however, begin a phase of life where their spiritual needs move toward center stage. This is where the yearning begins. At first it may be virtually undetectable like a faint whisper that gets drowned out by all the clutter of day-to-day living. In the beginning you may be aware of *something* but not be at all sure of what that something is. If you allow it, the yearning strengthens. You still may not be sure where the yearning leads, but you are sure that it exists. You know you are not imagining it. Of all the little voices that sound off in your head from time to time, you know this one deserves more respect than the others.

In her book *Awakening The Heroes Within*, Carol S. Pearson describes this process. "The call takes different forms for different people. Always the call is to function at a higher or deeper level, to find a way to live that has more significance and depth, to find out who you are beyond the social persona that you and your environment have jointly created." Some people hear it; some people feel it; others just come to know it. Some people search long and hard for their callings. Others prepare themselves to receive it and wait. Some use a combination of the two approaches. Native Americans, for instance, used the vision quest to find their path. During this ritual a young man would go into the wilderness and find a spot — he did not keep wandering — and wait. He could not come back to the tribe until he acquired his name and his vision. His name was given to him by the spirits, who told him essentially who he was.[1]

The idea of learning your name as part of the process of finding your calling is an important thought. Author and psychologist James Hillman makes the point that "only God knows our real names." This idea has been around since who-knows-when and it suggests that we may be called by a name other than the one we were given at birth. Instead we may be called by the sound of human suffering or the feel of injustice. Our spiritual name may be the dream of music not yet written or medical cures not yet discovered. When you encounter life at a "higher or deeper level" and you feel as if your name is being called, it may well be. You find out who you are when you awaken to what you need to do.

It's a tribute to the strength of our callings how many people in our world today feel their yearning. After all, we left the vision quests years ago out on the prairies. We've not replaced them. The idea that we are called to our own special missions has received neither attention nor respect from our culture. The idea has been practically ignored. Yet the yearning continues to move people. It would be an easier adjustment if folks were prepared for it. But even without this preparation, many many people move gracefully on to the road that leads to who they are meant to be. It's as if something within us understands what is taking place in spite of the fact that our culture has neglected this essential process. One can't help but wonder how many more souls would find their way if we lived in a time when we, as a culture, acknowledged and respected the process of receiving a calling.

So much of the identity confusion present today is related to the fact that large numbers of us don't understand the spiritual dimension of our personal identities. We feel the yearning but hesitate or try to avoid it when we cannot define it. Without an understanding of the process, these unexpected urges can lead us to believe that we are losing control. We like our control. We want to choose who we will be, so much so that we now have a huge industry of mental health gurus who assure us that who we are and what we will be happy with is completely up to us. When direction comes from someplace that we cannot manipulate, we may fear for our sanity. In order to restore our beloved control, we repress, deny, and turn to experts who assure us that we are pulling all our own strings.

No matter how hard you try, though, you can't give away your strings. Some of your strings are not yours to give away. You don't choose your purpose in life. It is an opportunity given to you to improve the world. It will likely have its challenges and its pain but it will also offer the kind of triumph you could not otherwise know. No one is called to a life where the contributions are insignificant. Your purpose is where your passion is. Although early on people sometimes resist their callings because the work does not seem important enough, the value becomes clear. You can't feel the power until you are willing to touch the power.

Once you feel the yearning, your personality must move to accommodate it. You need to be a certain way in order to fulfill your mission. Leaders must adjust their personalities accordingly. So too must builders, growers, teachers, healers, etc. You need to develop the character to carry forth your purpose. Change can be frightening and this is no exception. The changes you make in yourself may not endear you to the group that you once fought so hard to impress. You may be criticized and rejected. Sometimes your calling pulls you out into the desert all by yourself. Those who are unwilling to emerge fight the feeling that drives them toward their own unique journeys.

Those who are not aware of their own special journeys are those who inevitably become followers. Even when they are on the soapbox screaming the loudest, they are followers. Because they lack their own vision, they have nowhere to go. Without their own vision they retreat to the crowd and do what it takes to maintain refuge there. Here people may find structure and security, but if they never emerge to pursue their visions, they never achieve an identity of their own. They will never know the glory of walking their own road.

You will never know who you are until you allow yourself to see your vision and then be willing to emerge from the tribe and walk toward that vision. As your identity unfolds you develop a sense of what/who/how you need to be. The qualities you need to reach your vision all have their potential within you. This potential becomes real as you travel the road to you. Your calling will ultimately lead you back to a community but not until you have emerged as a person of character, a person capable of going into the desert alone.

Connecting with your calling is much more than an intellectual phenomenon. Emotions play a significant part as well. It's not unusual for people to fear it when they first hear it. But the curiosity can be so strong that the exploration continues anyway. Fear has its roots in ignorance, and curiosity is the antidote to ignorance. The fear of a calling does not go away by itself. Rather, it leaves as it is understood. As the fear leaves, wonder grows. Appreciation then sets in. If we stay with it, the appreciation evolves into gratitude. Those with the gratitude attitude live in a healthy state of mind. They are grateful for their callings. They are grateful for their lives.

In *Care for the Soul*, Thomas Moore points to another way the emotion arises in our relationship with our callings. "We like to think that we have chosen our work," he writes, "but it could be more accurate to say that our work has found us. Most people can tell fate-filled stories of how they happened to be in their current 'occupation.' These stories tell how the work came to occupy them, to take residence. Work is a vocation: we are called to it. But we can also be loved by our work. It can excite us, comfort us, and make us feel fulfilled."

A calling leads us to more than a job. It calls us to a life. A job may create an interest. But the life you are meant to live creates a yearning. It's not about how you will spend your time; it's about how you will make your contributions. And as Moore wisely instructs, it is about finding the work that will love you. This is important because we often think of looking for a vocation that we can learn to love. With a calling, however, the love is reciprocated. We can feel embraced by our missions. This love is part of the calling's voice. You move toward your calling by moving toward the love.

This need not be a complicated process. Buckminster Fuller believed that we begin to connect with our mission by simply asking ourselves, "What needs to be done?" Some people see it and then feel it. Others feel it first. Still others hear the first signs of their yearning or learn it in a dream. If you follow it, though, they all come together. The pieces start to focus and the energy builds. The various parts of your life start to assemble, all on the same track. The track points you in your direction as you follow the yearning to your purpose in life.

A good example of this might be Lacey, a sixty-two-year-old foster mother. Lacey takes in some of the most "hard to place" children in eastern Missouri. Lacey began taking in foster children after the last of her own left home. When I met her she had long since forgotten how many foster children she had given homes. It was her most recent placement, however, that caused her path to cross with mine.

She brought seven-year-old Darren for counseling after a psychological evaluation found him to have a rather severe case of attention deficit disorder with hyperactivity. Darren had reached the point where he couldn't control his environment and his environment couldn't control him. Interestingly, Lacey could control him better than any medication or mental health professional could.

Darren's life had been far from stable. He bounced through several foster placements. He had also lived for a time with his mother and a series of her boyfriends. One of these boyfriends sexually abused Darren over a period of months. As if this were not enough for a child to have endured, the Division of Family Services had just contacted Lacey to inform her that the man who had abused Darren had recently been diagnosed HIV positive. The state had already arranged for Darren to be tested for AIDS. In their hurry to get this arranged, though, no one realized that he had been scheduled to be tested on his eighth birthday.

I asked Lacey what she would do if Darren were HIV positive. Without a moment's hesitation and in a calm confident voice she replied, "I'll keep him with me until the state decides he needs special medical care." My first impulse was to remind her of all the cuts and scrapes she could expect from a young man as active as Darren. But she knew what was involved. It just didn't change her direction.

After we spoke for awhile, I asked Lacey why she does it. Why after raising her own children would she devote herself so thoroughly to these challenging kids?

"I just thought I'm supposed to help," she answered in a peaceful voice. "Once you decide to let yourself help, the Lord guides you to where you need to be." End of explanation. She *knew*. If you don't understand, more words won't help.

Then off they went, the sixty-two-year-old hero and the seven-year-old who may acquire an AIDS diagnosis for his birthday.

YOUNG PERSON, OLD PERSON

The yearning can begin at any time. Although it appears to arrive more often after mid-adolescence, young children sometimes feel it. It might seem that this would be confusing to a child who is even less prepared for it than adults. But, surprisingly, children who feel the yearning often handle it better than grown-ups. Many children who hear their callings relate to them in a natural way, almost as if they had been expecting them. They don't dissect it to the point of absurdity. They tend not to rip it apart for the sake of understanding it. They, instead, encounter it as a whole. Children know intuitively that their visions are more than the sum of their parts. We can learn about the biological world by dissecting it. We can even learn some things about our psychological world by isolating and separating its pieces. But the spiritual world is different. We come to know this world by encountering it in its totality. Children are better at this than most adults. Until adults find their childlike nature (i.e., their innocence), their spirituality will be incomplete. They will only have pieces.

Children love the feeling of awe. They gladly allow themselves to revel in it, stay with it, draw pictures of it, tell stories about it, and, finally, be grateful for it. Because they are comfortable with awe, they can see all the really big things in life. They can see the sunsets, the full moon, and the newborn anything. They look at the ocean and see every fish in it. And they let their feelings be as big as they really are. This comfort with the feeling of awe is essential to anyone who hopes to encounter the grandeur of life. To look at a lake and see much more than the surfaces or gaze at a mountain and see beyond the rocks, all this requires the freedom to feel awe. If this freedom is too frightening, we will focus on a few pieces and thus control our feelings. If we will not feel awe, maybe we will permit ourselves to have the more controlled feeling of, say, being "interested." Being interested can lead us to knowledge about the body and it can also lead us to learn some things about the mind. But in order to understand the spiritual side of life, we have to free ourselves to feel awe.

Another reason children gracefully respond to yearnings is that they are not as interested in an identity as adults are. If children hear a certain path calling, they may not have to abandon an entire identity that was created to walk in a different direction. Children do not face the situation where they have prepared themselves for years to be an attorney only to find themselves being pulled toward the healing arts. Hearing a calling early in life may help a person find a straighter path to his destination. (Keep in mind that what may at the time appear as a detour may actually be a part of one's calling.)

I do not know how it is determined when a calling will be sent. I suppose at least part of this depends on what you believe is the source of the calling. Some people report finding their direction early in life while others don't feel the guidance until much later. Some who find it late in life say, retrospectively, that it was always there but that they wouldn't let themselves hear it. Others disagree. Lacey believes that we are called by God. Others aren't so sure. It seems we must answer for ourselves *where* the yearning begins and how it is determined *when* it will begin.

Carol S. Pearson summarizes what I believe is our culture's thinking on when the yearning's most likely to start. She says that while it can come at any age, "it is clearest and most distinct in late adolescence and early adulthood. This is the time of exploration — exploring new lands, new ideas, new experiences — the time to learn about the world. It is a time for travel, for study, for experimentation."[2] If our yearning comes from our biological make-up or our psyche, then this is certainly the most likely time to find one's true preferences. There is, hopefully, enough independence to act upon one's own view of the world, enough support to encourage one to become who one truly is, and enough freedom to make the moves one believes are right. If this is the case, then all the cylinders have fallen into place at the right time. It is as if it were planned this way, as if we built much of our culture around the understanding that we receive our direction during early adulthood.

Psychologically, this appears true. Early adulthood is a time of life when society says: "It's time to decide what you will do and who you will be. We give you some freedom and some support but you must decide, and soon." Perhaps more than at any other period in life, the young adult is given the support of his community to feel the yearning.

Just because psychological variables such as social support contribute to one's willingness (and consequently one's ability) to hear a calling does not necessarily prove that callings are psychological entities. A person can be more psychologically prepared at one point in his life to feel the yearning than he may be at another. Our minds and our emotions can close down or make so much noise that it becomes difficult to feel the yearning, hear the calling, see the vision. Or our feelings and psyches can open themselves to what life has to offer. It is in these states, however we reach them, that we are most receptive to the guidance of the spiritual world.

This receptivity can occur at any time. Our culture may indeed be most cooperative at a certain point in the life-span and therefore more people may feel their yearning for the first time during this age. But the calling can begin any time. Beyond this, one calling may build upon another so that a calling of youth may serve as the foundation for a new vision that arrives in mid-life.

When the yearning arrives it can bring painful decisions with it. It may ask you to leave behind an identity that you have sworn allegiance to. It may drive you back to square one to start over in an unfamiliar arena, one that does not have the room or the need for the laurels you've already collected. Above all, once you acknowledge the yearning, once you allow it to really touch you, you will be forever changed. Even if you choose to fight it and never act on it, it will have changed you. You will have seen your road — the one that exists for you alone, the road that will lead you and love you and ultimately make you grateful. Even the momentary glimpse is an experience too powerful to repress completely. Once you know your direction, you never completely forget it.

Reaching your true self may take time. Jazz great Miles Davis once said, "Sometimes you have to play a long time, to play like yourself." We could just as easily replace the word "play" with almost any other quality such as build, speak, lead, write, manage, parent, or grow. From the point when you begin to feel the yearning your life is changed. Generally speaking, there are two responses you can make to your calling. First, you can refuse. If you choose this option, then you live with the guilt that comes with presenting a false self to the world. If you decide to go this way, you will be living a lie. You can repress the awareness of this deceit but your repression will never hide the facts completely. The truth will surface time and again and, each time it does, it will remind you of the lie.

And even though repression is a far from perfect solution, it requires huge amounts of mental energy, energy that could be spent building a healthy, productive, honest life. It takes energy to bury the truth. Thus we have a situation where a great deal of energy is spent in the service of a process that harms you.

The healthier alternative is clear. The yearning represents a call to be the person you are meant to be. When it first reaches you it may be frightening or, perhaps, disappointing. It may feel like more than you can handle or it may be a message to become something you feel is beneath you. Your calling may first ask you to strengthen your confidence or its first demand may be that you find your humility.

Your decision represents the first step in finding the real you. The yearning invites you to a journey, a journey with a very real destination. Your first step is your decision to follow the yearning. If you decide to honor your yearning, there will be other steps on the road to you. While everyone travels this path in their own way, there are aspects of this journey that seem common to those who seek to find the life they are called to. In the next chapter we will consider the first step: the decision to honor your yearning. If you choose to do so, you will then encounter the dragon(s), the shadow, fellow travelers and teachers, insight, doubt, innocence, humility, empowerment, enlightenment, and then finally, your arrival.

How long does it take to travel the road to you? As long as you need. And when you arrive, you will be the person you need to be to fulfill your calling. You will be the person you are meant to be.

CONCLUSION

The road to you begins with the understanding and the feeling that you have a destination. This destination may not be crystal clear at first but it is real enough to set your sights. You may not know the details but you realize that there is somewhere you need to be, something you need to do.

Many self-help philosophies say that the journey is more important than the destination. Others go so far as to suggest that there is no destination at all, only a journey. While I believe that many people do wander aimlessly through life, these individuals are not on a path to knowing themselves. If there is no destination — or if the destination were not important — the journey would not be worth the effort. Because the destination is so valuable, however, it motivates one to walk through the pain and heartache that can arise along the way. Please understand, the journey is not all misery. There is joy, enthusiasm, discovery, intimacy, and triumph included in your sojourn. But there will also be disappointment, frustration, sorrow, fear, and confusion. We walk through the hard times because we have accepted our yearning to be what we are meant to be. Your destination on this journey, then, is the real you.

CHAPTER TWO

THE DECISION

Deep down inside we all want to be significant. We want our lives to count for something. We don't need to climb *the* Mount Everest but we need to climb our own Mount Everest. Our mountains come to us in the form of a yearning. Once we see the foot of the mountain, we are faced with the decision whether or not we will ascend it.

This decision is the most important move we make in life. It is our psychological and spiritual birth. Unlike physical birth, which is orchestrated by forces outside of ourselves, this birth is the result of an active deliberate choice. If we accept our yearning and move to actualize it, we are born into the life that we are meant to live. This is the life where we become truly significant because we will contribute what only we can. If, however, we choose not to pursue the yearning, we remain unborn. We live a life written and produced by someone else. We might have the security of life in the womb, but we will never experience the exhilaration of life on the mountaintop.

Deciding to walk your own path gives you life. It is the essence of psychological and spiritual health. Until you make this decision, you will be imprisoned by your security. You will not be living your life. Instead, you will live an endless series of shoulds, oughts, and musts created by other people. If you never follow your calling you will never know your Higher Power. You will, at best, know stories about God told by people who may only know stories themselves. If you act on your yearning, however, you will move toward its source. You can find the force that calls you. If you follow your calling, you will experience its source.

You will have to decide what it is you experience. People who follow their visions frequently reach a force they identify as God. The God they find, though, may be quite different from the God they thought they knew.

There can be a world of difference between what you see when you connect with God and what you knew of Him through the stories you were told. This applies to both believers and non-believers. Many atheists don't understand what they refuse to believe. It's not always God they don't believe in; it's the stories they've been told about Him that don't seem real. In order to believe, they have to move beyond other people's stories. Like believers, they have to move to the place where they can see for themselves if there is a God to believe in.

The decision to follow the yearning is the decision to become the real you. Understanding is not enough. Action is required. Following the yearning requires movement. Thought may be private but movement is public. Every step is a declaration of independence. No one's mission, no one's identity is found in conformity alone. During this decision-making stage, there may be intense conflict between your need to belong and your need to be significant. Significance means emerging from the group on your own personal vision quest to find who you are. Even if you return to the group, you will do so as a contributor and not just as a conformer. You will be empowered. You will have your own identity and mission. You will be rewarded with the courage to stand on your own feet and remain tenaciously committed to the work that you know needs to be done.

In April, 1995, when the federal building in Oklahoma City was blown up and hundreds of lives were destroyed, thousands and thousands of people throughout the world followed a call to do what they could to repair the devastation in America's heartland. No one could turn back time. Success, no matter how amazing, would never be complete. While it appeared that evil had conquered all, people began to feel the yearning to contribute to the healing. In the end, triumph belonged to those who decided to follow the yearning. They walked into the face of disaster, faced the dragon and said, "I'm not going back!" Heroes and fatalities emerged from the rubble. If no one had followed the yearning, there would only have been death and destruction. If no one had followed the yearning, there would have been no heroes.

There are yearnings that pull you toward immediate action. Then there are yearnings that call you to the mission of your life. The people who moved decisively to do what needed to be done in Oklahoma City felt an immediate need. Even though their sacrifices were great, however, they had support that you may not. The entire nation rallied around this crisis. Rarely did someone risk rejection or disapproval because of the money they sent or the blood they donated. The yearning you feel may not lead to such acceptance. You may be called to do things that take you to unpopular places. And you may be called to do them alone.

But if you listen hard enough, you may hear support for your decision to boldly travel your own path. This is the stuff commencement speeches and motivational talks are made of. When speakers are asked to motivate people they almost invariably hit this theme the hardest. If these orators are to be believed, it seems the most important decision you make in life is the decision to take charge of your life and dare to follow your dreams and become the person you are meant to be. These inspirational messages pass on the wisdom of the ages: Follow your calling rather than the crowd. Decide to follow the yearning you feel. As Joseph Campbell writes, "The big question is whether you are going to say a hearty yes to your adventure."

Research on the psychology of regret has added some scientific data to support this. Studies have found that it is common in later life to feel the pangs of regret for dreams not followed. Also, interestingly enough, it is extremely rare to find people who regret having followed a dream.[1] Early in life we fear the risks that lie ahead of us. Later in life we regret not having taken them.

The decision phase of the road to you is perhaps the most crucial. The yearning (first stage) comes to you whether you care for it or not and even your most diligent efforts to repress it will never be completely effective. But the decision requires deliberate movement. Many people spend their lives avoiding this. They feel the pull to a life mission but they spend their days fighting the yearning. They keep their callings a secret. They pay the price of guilt and regret but they prefer this to the fear that comes with climbing their mountain.

Becoming who you are meant to be requires that you walk through some fear. But with each step you become more committed to the journey. This is why I say that the decision stage may be the most crucial. Once a decision is made to act, a momentum begins that helps carry you through the fear and doubt. Once the decision is made to follow the yearning, the momentum begins to surge. This energy that starts with the first step, grows with each subsequent step. If the first step is never made, the journey never begins.

This first step may be described as emerging from the cocoon. It is often a public declaration of who you believe you are. At this point, all that energy that may have been used to repress your yearning can now be applied to its service. The fear may still be there — and if it's not, it will reappear sooner or later — but now you have the energy and determination to get started.

FEAR

In order to accomplish anything significant, you must walk your way through fear. It's our reluctance to deal with fear, more than anything else, that keeps us from plunging into our great adventure. The fear will be there. Don't let it surprise you. Don't let it come out of the dark. Put a light on it. And above all, don't think that you're the only one who feels it. All courageous people do. The only ones who don't feel it are the ones who don't take the risks. (You know, the ones who regret it later.)

Fear is a predictable experience. It arises whenever you strive to reach your potential. Fear reminds you how easily you can fail and of all the catastrophic consequences that might result from this failure. Fear might even remind you of your mortality and how easily body parts tear, bruise, and break. This sort of thing keeps many of us frozen, not daring to move.

When you make your decision to pursue your vision, you are committing yourself to live with a certain amount of fear. This isn't necessarily all gloom and doom. You can turn fear into positive energy such as productivity, creativity, and humor. Fear is a form of energy that can hold you back or drive you forward. You control its use.

It is a mistake to assume that fear has to be an enemy. It can be one of your finest allies. One of the most destructive beliefs you can carry is the idea that fear is only an obstacle, one that needs to be destroyed or avoided. In truth, fear is a great motivator. Thoreau wrote, "If thou art a writer, write as if thy time is short." He knew that the anxiety provoked by our mortality is a life force. He knew that the awareness of death can bring people to life.

The avoidance of fear is the avoidance of life. In order to be the person you are meant to be you must be willing to walk into those frightening caves that you will encounter on your journey. My friend and colleague William L. White describes the writer's journey this way: "The great writers all wander up to the opening of the dark cave and do battle with the voices that say, 'Stay in the light. If you venture in here, we'll kill you!'"[2] These voices always seem to hover around the beginnings of new experiences. Until we conquer the fear, we are not worthy of what lies beyond.

Perhaps the most important lesson we learn during the decision phase of our journey is how to turn fear into power. The formula for making this transformation varies to some extent. Everyone who turns fear into power includes his or her own unique chemistry in the process. Some do it quickly and decisively. Others let the potion brew and the heat build. There are, however, similarities — steps taken by all those who transform fear into power.

First, you must allow yourself to feel the fear. Fear gets angry and destructive when we force it into our dungeons. We begin to understand the power of our fears when we hold them before us. We start to free ourselves from the tyranny of our fears when we seize them. Once we feel the fear, we can move to the second essential step — identifying the fear. With so many fears out there, this can be a task. Like many significant tasks, at first it may seem impossible. Your fear may be the fear of death, rejection, disappointment, ridicule, failure, love, or intimacy. It may take a friend or a counselor to help you identify your fear. Identifying your fear is complicated by the fact that it is often the thing that is most vile to you and thus the last thing you want to look at. Still, you must identify it. The most common reason fear remains in our lives is that we have not identified it correctly.

Third, you must name your fear. You will know its name because it will feel right when you use it. Once you name your fear you will feel the first signs of its power working for you. You are now starting to harness the power of fear. By naming your fear you have a way to address it. You can retrieve it when it tries to hide deep in your psyche. And even when it seeks to rule the day, if you've named it correctly, it cannot dominate you.

Once you've correctly named your fear you are ready to move on to the fourth and final step in the process of turning fear into power. Now you must address your fear. Addressing it brings it further into the light. You may want to vent a bit. You may attack it for oppressing you as long as it has. There might be any number of things you want to say to your fear. But there is one thing that you must say. There is one essential issue that you must settle with your fear before you let it go. When you address your fear you must insist that it teach you something. All fears have something important to teach. Unfortunately, many people live with fear all their lives without finding its lesson. Equally unfortunate are all those souls who have outgrown fears without collecting the wisdom they possess. Life is much too short to waste these precious learning opportunities. Your fears, the things you want to avoid most, may contain the knowledge you need most.

If you fear rejection, for example, look it in the face and say, "Fear of rejection, what do you have to teach me?" It's that simple. Don't make it complicated. Complicating this only serves to help you avoid it. If you are asking, "What could a fear of rejection possibly teach me?" I might suggest that this fear might teach you how important relationships are or how easy it is to hurt someone. The fear of rejection could help you learn to appreciate people whom you are taking for granted. Ironically, the fear of rejection that keeps you shy, withdrawn, and isolated may contain the lesson of how much you need intimacy. The fear of rejection may teach you about loneliness, friendship, human pain, or put you in touch with parts of you that you didn't know existed.

Once you have felt your fear, identified it, named it, and have begun to address it, hold on to it until you extract its lesson. Every fear that blocks your path has a lesson. If you are afraid to move on your calling, speak to that fear by name. Speak to it directly. If you are afraid that people will think you are crazy then speak to that fear too. But never release the fear until it has shared its lessons. Only then will you internalize the full power of the fear.

Of the four stages, stage number two (identifying the fear) can be especially difficult when the fear relates to one's calling. Our culture has largely neglected the idea of a calling so it is not unusual that people get confused when we feel the yearning. Issues surrounding a calling would be easier to identify if we were prepared for them. But typically we are not, so when they arrive we tend to mis-identify them. We may describe the fear of our callings as anxiety, depression, or agitation. Or we may label it by how it manifests itself behaviorally, such as addiction. We use these words, as incorrect as they may be, because they are part of the language we have been taught. If you've never learned that we can fear our callings and that this fear can cripple us emotionally and spiritually, you may have a particularly difficult time identifying it in yourself.

Remember, the process of taking the power from fear begins when you allow yourself to feel it. By doing so you bring the fear into the light. At this point the fear is much easier to identify. When you name your fear you begin to understand its power. The transformation of power completes itself as you address your fear directly. When you address it, you can tell it or ask it anything you want. It is essential, however, that you hold on to the fear until you learn what it has to teach you.

With this in mind, we can answer the pivotal question: Why is fear an inevitable part of growth? Working through fear is thought to be a rite of passage needed to build character. This strength of character supports growth and the development of values. While this is certainly true, we now know that there is more to it. Fear not only *prepares* you for your journey, it also *helps point the way.* Fear teaches. Fear helps put you in touch with what matters to you. In so doing it serves as a guidepost for your journey in life.

DISCONTENT AND THE WARRIOR WITHIN

At times, your calling may be spoken most clearly through the voice of discontent. That angry sound that increases its volume as you become more deeply entrenched in places where you don't belong can taunt you unmercifully. It can also save your life. Like fear, discontent is a guide that we may not want to look at. Because it makes uncomfortable demands on us, we tend to avoid it. Avoiding it, of course, doesn't make it go away. In fact, avoidance fuels discontent. It becomes as loud as it has to in order to be heard.

Carl Jung believed that each of us has a warrior within us that helps us defend ourselves as well as defeat the dragons that block our life's path. The warrior is a protector. If we accept it into our lives, it will fight to keep us safe and destroy the obstacles that stand between us and our destination. If, however, we deny the warrior and refuse to accept it into our lives, the warrior turns against us and uses its considerable power to try to destroy us. The warrior would prefer to support and defend you, but if you don't let it, you will find yourself fighting what should be a powerful ally.

Jung claimed that the warrior is an archetype. An archetype is a deep and abiding pattern in the human psyche that remains powerful and present over time.[3] It is a story that becomes a psychological force.

I believe Jung's notion of an internal warrior is quite useful. The role of the warrior has long been a part of humankind. Literature across cultures and time is replete with tales of the warrior. Furthermore, I am not aware of any civilization that has survived for any length of time that has not recognized and utilized the warrior. The warrior is so fundamental to civilization, that over time it has become a part of who we are.

The question then becomes: why? Why do we need an internal warrior? One explanation would be that like other living creatures we need to be able to protect ourselves. In order to insure self-preservation we need the skills to do so. The warrior personifies these qualities. But there is another reason each of us houses a warrior. In everyone's life there will be obstacles. Obstacles will stand in the way of happiness, intimacy, and finding one's mission. In order to become all that you're capable of, you must be able to rise to a challenge. Some people love their warriors so much that they let them run their lives. For these people, life is one long fight. These fights may produce a certain number of conquests, but they will never lead to real happiness. Then there are other individuals who disdain their warriors. They imprison them deep within themselves. Such persons will not ask the warrior for help. Consequently, they will live a peaceful life but will be routinely pushed around by forces that would keep them from the places they need to be. And, if Jung was correct, a warrior that cannot use its power to be helpful will turn its energies against the person it exists to help.

We need the warrior energy within us if we are to do the things we are called to do. We are called to be significant. Being significant requires that we honor the warrior within us. We should use it when we need it and put it away when we do not. The warrior is but one aspect of our being and should be treated as such. The warrior does not need to be king. It does, however, need our respect. The respected warrior can peacefully await its time.

Often, the warrior is awakened by the voice of discontent. Discontent arises when we are in a place that no longer feels right. And even though these feelings may be piercing, we feel stuck, unable or unwilling to make the changes needed to ease our pain. It is not uncommon that one must struggle to remove one's discontent. One example of this is the person who hates his job but would rather stay chained to the mountain of discontent than take the risk to change his situation. He elects to remain safe and miserable, volunteering for a life that will never make him happy, a life where he will never feel significant.

As the voice of discontent gets louder, it awakens the warrior. The warrior leads the fight that keeps us true to ourselves. It leads the charge that returns us to our proper paths. The warrior storms through the fear that locks us in misery. Sometimes it helps us make corrections. Sometimes it helps us make changes. It shouldn't control us. But if we let it, it can help us.

So what happens when someone hears and feels the shrill scream of discontent but refuses to make the appropriate changes? Well, Jung insisted that if the warrior is not allowed to help the individual, the warrior will turn its force against that person. So it is that the fellow who hates his job but who dares not make the necessary changes develops ulcers, heart problems, depression, angry outbursts, or marital problems. All that personal power that he has within him to correct his situation explodes aimlessly inside of him. Among the casualties from this explosion is the love of life.

Unfortunately, because so few theories in psychology and psychiatry consider the possibility that we feel yearnings based in our callings, people who suffer from the pain and discontent of an unanswered calling are generally treated incorrectly. Too often mental health professionals make no effort to help their patients identify and connect with their callings. Callings don't always meet the requirements of "reality testing." So instead of focusing on bringing a calling into the light, psychotherapy often attempts to help people drown out the yearning. And when the warrior comes to the surface to help rescue the person from the therapist, this is diagnosed as "resistance," something that must be "worked through." In this case, working through means looking for ways to kill the warrior.

We can be rational without our inner warrior. We can be in touch with our feelings without it (although those feelings will lack passion). Ironically, we may even be safer without the warrior. It's the warrior's task to help take us through the dangerous times and without it we may never leave our safe places, no matter how unhappy they make us. In short, we can be quite normal without the warrior.

If you follow your calling, however, you will be a great deal more than normal. You will be significant. You will be a contributor.

MOVEMENT

In spite of the fear, uncertainty, and any number of physical limitations, many people move to follow a yearning that only they can feel. They trust themselves enough to know that what they feel is authentic. They allow their courage to awaken and propel them to the places where they belong. Perhaps the greatest conquest in life is the first step in the right direction.

Sad to say, not everyone makes that step. Some spend their days living someone else's life. They never find and create themselves. They stay safe. These people never really understand when they hear others talk about happiness. In order to feel happiness, you have to let yourself feel. By living someone else's life you lose your ability to touch your own feelings. If you turn away from the yearning, you turn away from you.

When one begins to act on one's yearning, life begins to change. Someone once described this to me as the point "when all the colors come on." A world that was black and white with a lot of gray suddenly fills with greens and golds and blues and reds and every color you can imagine. Life unfolds as you decide to move closer to you.

Richard A. Heckler, in his interesting book *Waking Up, Alive*, points to this phenomenon in the lives of people who have made serious suicide attempts. His research followed people from their attempt through their recovery. One of his most important findings is the discovery that these people began their recovery once they decided to *move*. In most cases they changed their place of residence (which often involved a change in relationships). These moves also included changes in their work and school settings. Once these moves were made, many of Heckler's subjects left their "suicidal trance" and began a more spontaneous, authentic existence.

It seems that these individuals moved into their own worlds. They took charge of their lives and began to walk their own paths. Once on their own paths, they had a reason to live, they had a destination. When they found their road, they knew how to act. In many cases, creativity emerged with a force not seen before. As creativity is a manifestation of one's uniqueness, one might conclude that when someone finds her place, she becomes accepting, even proud (rather than ashamed), of the qualities that make her unique.

Making that first step is so important because it is through this move that you make your intentions known. Once we make a public statement (i.e., act) concerning what we want to do with our lives, our identities begin to take shape. We are out in the open and going back in may be difficult. Even if there is no support for your move, you will feel your power. If you are true to yourself, you will — perhaps for the first time — feel yourself supporting yourself. You may become so involved with your mission that you have no time, energy, or inclination to eye those who may criticize your efforts. This is freedom — the psychological equivalent of flying. As soon as you take the first step you are rewarded with the power and permission to be the best teacher or mayor in the history of the world.

It's not enough to think in a new way. Your yearning pulls you to do something. You are called to act. Your life won't improve if all you do is talk to a sympathetic ear and/or read self-help books. You have to take action. Similarly, I doubt the people who wrote the Bible meant it to be an intellectual exercise. More likely, they hoped it would help people live better lives.

When people begin to move, they come to understand this quickly. Everything about it feels right. When you finally stand up and say, "I am going to run for union representative," you may feel fear, but if this is part of your mission you will also feel right. Likewise, you will feel empowered when you drop the letter you wrote to the editor of the newspaper in the mailbox. Empowerment is your reward for taking that first step. It then grows with each subsequent step.

Some have suggested that this is the point when miracles begin. Goethe, for instance, once wrote:

> There is one elementary Truth — the ignorance of which kills countless ideas and splendid plans: The moment one definitely commits oneself, then Providence moves, too. All sorts of things occur to help one that would never otherwise have occurred.

Dostoyevsky penned, "Taking a new step, uttering a new word is what people fear most." Taking those first steps is often an act of faith. No one else feels your yearning. There's no way to do scientific verification here. You move because deep inside you feel a need to move. It's much more than a whim. It's the road opening up before you. You are, however, the only one who sees your road. Seeing the road may be your first miracle. Once you step on to it there may be more. Whoever said, "Leap and the net will appear," knew that we sometimes have to take that first step before we see the net. One might go as far as to suggest that you can't see it because it isn't there. It's not there until *after* you decide to move.

I realize that it's not always as easy as it sounds. If you sit in the fear of taking that first step for too long, you can come to feel paralyzed. At that point it can seem as though you are unable to move anywhere. Discontent may be exploding inside you and your warrior (your potential ally) has turned against you. Your warrior may be attacking your body from within and hammering away at your psyche with an unending barrage of discouragement, depression, or fear.

The mental health profession has developed a wide variety of strategies for dealing with this situation. Most, unfortunately, have missed the mark completely. These failed therapies have, for the most part, focused on insisting that patients repeat in endless detail every facet of their turmoil. Rather than helping people take the first step, they give them reasons to remain stuck. The only comfort here, short term though it may be, stems from the fact that the patient no longer feels responsible for his being stuck. He comes to feel that he is the product of his story. Less responsibility, less guilt. Maybe it helps for awhile if one's pain is someone else's fault.

Not much comes from examining one's life if one is unwilling to move. For many people the therapeutic experience they need most is one that frees them to move. There are so many ways to make this happen. But it seems that everyone must find the experience that is most effective for them. Sometimes a person can be freed through walking, dancing, aerobics, or almost any form of exercise. These activities rejuvenate a person to the extent that they can fill him with the power of movement. This is why physical exercise has been found to ease a variety of emotional complaints. As you learn to move and feel the power of movement, you gain more control of your life.

When the person who is stuck begins to move, the fear

becomes replaced by euphoria. This is the feeling of being truly alive. It's like walking in the mountains, swimming in the ocean, or dancing in your bare feet. It's the feeling of being empowered to become what you are meant to be. It is a psychological and spiritual birth. It's the point where you awaken and become fully alive.

This euphoria, as wonderful and powerful as it is, does not last forever. If you decide to follow your yearning, you will know times of great happiness. But you will also, likely, experience sorrow and suffering. Not all your experiences on the road to you will be pleasant. But with each step you become more empowered. Sometimes you will be a conqueror and other times merely a survivor. In either case, you will be something significant.

It has been suggested by some that we fear making important life moves when we are confused about our identities. More often than not, this theory is incorrect. We don't stay paralyzed because we are confused about our identities; we remain confused about who we are until we begin to move. We need to move on what we believe and feel before we will ever know who we are. The intellectual trap many of us fall into is the mistaken notion that it is unhealthy to make any moves until we really know who we are.

In order to grow you must be willing to move before you have all the answers. Those first steps may be steps of faith made in response to a yearning that no one else can see or feel. Discovering who you are meant to be requires that you make the decision to follow your calling. The decision is not made until the movement begins. Thought and emotion are meant to lead to action. If they do not lead to action, they will turn into guilt — guilt for turning away from the life you are called to.

ENTHUSIASM

Those who decide to move in the direction of their callings are greeted with a surge of energy. An abundance of power from within rushes to the surface to pull you and drive you further along your way. Moving in your true direction leads to the liberation of the soul. With this liberation comes courage, motivation, and a deeper, more profound love for life. Once the soul is liberated it fills one's entire being. Now the person is no longer governed by physical and psychological rules. He is now, first and foremost, a spiritual being. He continues to have a body and a mind that must be tended to. But now these needs are secondary to the needs of his soul.

When the soul is liberated, one passes through a period of pleasant (even euphoric) instability. This is the feeling of falling in love with one's life. The best literary example I can think of would be Scrooge on Christmas morning. While swimming in euphoria, as well as healthy insanity, he began to become the man he was meant to be. The chains were lifted and he liberated his soul. His bitterness gave way to an enthusiasm for love and for life. His selfishness was replaced with generosity and he became a decent man.

The power within you comes out to meet your mission. This is an important indicator that you are doing the work that you have been called to do. When energy becomes available that previously did not seem to exist, this may be a sign that you are doing what you need to do.

After you move into your calling you may look back with a smile and realize that you now love what you once feared. Love is the essence of the enthusiasm one feels at this point in life. So even though it's still early on the road to you, you have already learned and accomplished much. Once you feel love for your mission, you have learned a great deal about yourself. To a large extent, *we are what we love.*

CONCLUSION

First, callings ask to be heard. Once we acknowledge and accept our yearning we encounter the calling's second request — movement. There are obstacles in the way of this movement. Yet one of the most important lessons one learns during this time is that every obstacle has a lesson. In order to transcend the obstacles in life, you need knowledge, power, and a passion for learning. If you accept your calling, you receive knowledge. If you act on your calling, you receive power and passion.

Although a person's journey is far from over at this point, once movement begins, much has been accomplished. A force has been set in motion that will gain power as it goes. With each step it becomes harder to go back to where one began.

Once you have worked through the fear and put yourself in motion, euphoria arrives. It's as if this is how you are rewarded for taking those first steps. Although the euphoria does not last forever, this is an extremely important phase.

It pulls you further along the road to you.

CHAPTER THREE

THE DRAGON

Dragons pervade mythology. They have been written into the tales of cultures from around the world in spite of the fact that they have never walked this earth. They are symbols of adversity. Dragons threaten life and limb as they stand between the traveler and his destination. Fierce enough to frighten the most dauntless soul, they are easily misunderstood. The dragons you face in life may have more to offer than a fight. They may be prepared to share strength and wisdom.

When Nietzsche wrote, "If it doesn't kill me, it makes me stronger," I'm sure he was talking about dragons. This is the kind of adversity that is capable of destroying you. It's the failure, the loss, the humiliation. It's the illness, the injury, the disability. The dragon is symbolic of the adversity that comes to you from an external source. You didn't bring it with you on your journey; it rose up to meet you. It has an unpredictable nature and appears to have an evil intent. If we think only at the primitive level, we can see only two alternatives — run from it or kill it. A more enlightened person, however, realizes other choices.

It is an unfortunate fact. The road to you passes through adversity. Sometimes you will have to swim against the tide or even up a waterfall. You may have to sail against a hurricane or leave a group of people who mean everything to you. Adversity, you see, is part of the path. Life can and should be a wonderful experience but it is not without pain. Even when you live a good life, there will be hurt and sadness.

You may be stunned to see your first dragon. After having made the decision to follow your yearning you may have been filled with enthusiasm. And after having struggled with that decision to move, you may have thought it would be all downhill from there. Then, just when everything seems wonderful, adversity strikes. At first it may not seem real. Then it may seem like it is all a mistake, that something like this was never intended for you, and that if you wait it out it will disappear. But you wait, and it doesn't.

Your dragons are part of your path. How you deal with them will determine what comes next. How your dragons are chosen is a mystery that you are probably not yet ready to solve. You may not be able to figure this out until you have found the source of your calling. When you find one, you may find the other. Keep in mind, though, that not all your questions will be answered in this lifetime.

The dragon may place any number of demands on you. Different dragons will push you to develop different dimensions of yourself. In each case, you need to develop a new skill in order to survive. This is a demand that all dragons make — that you grow. It's not enough to survive. If you only survive, then the dragon has killed you. In order to conquer your dragon you must survive with your soul intact. This means that in order to continue on your journey in life, you must deal with the dragon in an honorable way and learn from this experience. If you do not — even if you survive — neither your character nor your self-respect will be strong enough to carry you toward your destination.

Nowhere is this problem more evident than in people who live with addictions. Addictions are repetitious behaviors that serve to keep someone from dealing with a difficult reality. People can become addicted to alcohol, drugs, food, gambling, shopping, and a variety of other behaviors. People with addictions typically have a history of surviving their dragons through anesthesia. They numb or distract themselves to the point where they don't feel the wounds inflicted by their dragons. Many, but not all, survive the onslaught, but they do not do so with a healthy soul. They survive through escape, never moving forward or growing. It's not until they look honestly into the face of adversity that they begin to work toward recovery.

A dragon can be anything that forces you to change your story. Each of us carries a story inside us. This story is an explanation of the ways of life. The story describes many things including what we see as our place in the world. Good stories are open to change. As we age they grow richer, deeper. If our stories prepare us for change, we are less likely to be overwhelmed by it. If, however, our stories are arrogant and rigid, they are ill-equipped to handle adversity. In this case, the dragon creates a therapeutic crisis: grow or be destroyed.

Unlike storybooks, the tale does not end when the dragon is killed. In real life, you may not need to kill your monster. And no matter how you deal with it, your story is far from over when you move beyond the dragon. How you deal with the dragon prepares you for what lies beyond.

The dragon always demands that you grow. Some believe that the dragon can only challenge you to a fight and that the only possible victory is to destroy it. Such a sad misconception this is. The dragon stands before you and asks, "What will you do with me?" Some dragons you kill, others you walk around, others leave if you stare them down. Some dragons you need to tame. Others you must ask to teach you.

People have a tendency to move in only one direction. They tend to kill all their dragons or run from each one that crosses their path. If the only quality you've developed is speed, you tend to do a lot of running. If the only quality you have is a sword, you tend to do a lot of fighting. The wisest of the wise study the dragon before they act. They grow strategies to seize the day.

Dragons, on the other hand, have their own tendencies. They usually insist that you develop a new skill to deal with each of them. (After all, if your old skills worked, it wouldn't be much of a dragon.)

Although you may not have to kill your dragon, you do need to survive it and pass beyond it with honor. In so doing you will have conquered your monster. Through this conquest you will have made a commitment to the road to you. You will have met adversity, looked it in the eye, survived it, and moved on with your soul intact. Taking a risk is an essential element in the process of making a commitment. One who is unwilling to risk is incapable of commitment. Taking this risk means you value what lies ahead (even though you cannot be completely certain what that may be).

Besides the uncertainty, there are the wounds. Even the conquests can leave scars. While we will discuss these wounds in more detail later, there is one important piece of psychological aftermath that needs attention here. Tragedy often leaves us with the gnawing question, "Why?" Among the variety of forms this question can take are: Why me? Why do these things have to happen? Why would God, if there is a God, want me to go through this?

When people speak such thoughts they are often met with advice such as: "It does no good to wonder why," or "There are no answers to why." People give this kind of advice in an effort to rescue someone they care for from the pain of their wounds. Wondering why can be frustrating. In the wake of a tragedy there seldom exists an acceptable answer to the question, "Why?"

Still, the question must be asked. A wounded person needs to wonder why. The fact that it is such a natural and universal response to tragedy suggests that it is part of our being and must be respected. The fact that asking why does not produce an immediate and perfect answer does not detract one iota from the value of the question. Asking why you were wounded is a beginning step in a necessary process. Like many other questions, this one has value long before it is resolved.

Determining why you have been wounded can be hampered by at least two issues. First, at the point you receive your wound you may be too filled with emotion to think clearly. Emotions cannot answer the question, "Why?" You must accept the emotions that come with being hurt, give them their time and then, and only then, can you possibly understand the meaning of your tragedy. Give feelings their time and respect, and reason will come in its own time.

Second, until you learn how to encounter the dragon you will not know how to thrive after being wounded. This is one of the dragon's lessons — how to survive your wounds. You must struggle with a wound before you can understand it. It is not until you accept the wound and own it as now being a part of you that you will allow it to speak to you and explain itself.

Wounds are inevitable in an encounter with the dragon. While it may be too early in your journey to understand why you have been hurt, it is important that you begin to ask why. Why me? Why now? Why suffering? Why life? As we hold these questions near to us, our spirit becomes deeper. You may not be at a place where you can answer these. But as we will see, humility precedes awakening. We have to accept not knowing before we can know.

The dragon brings questions with it. For better or for worse, it does not bring as many answers. In all its many forms, the dragon asks, "What will you do with me?" How you answer this will determine the course of your journey.

THE ENCOUNTER

People who feel the yearning and then make the decision to follow it, but who never face the dragon, will be forever starting their journey over. They return to their starting point, get up and begin again, only to turn around once more when they come upon misfortune. These folks hear a calling and decide, with all the best intentions, to grow in their true directions. They do well in the thinking, feeling, and talking stages but, for whatever reason, they cannot get through the resistance that comes to those who act. They move until they meet a dragon. Then they retreat and the process begins again.

Individuals who are constantly beginning again may display a variety of behaviors. At first they may be preoccupied with self-help literature. They sincerely want to grow but lack the piece that carries them through the hard times. They believe that reading and listening to tapes and attending lectures will prepare them for their encounter with life's adversities. They may learn every self-help skill imaginable but it's never enough. They collect so many weapons for killing their dragons that the weight of their weaponry alone makes it virtually impossible to move.

Until someone successfully deals with their first dragon they are easily led by the advice of others. Defeating the dragon is an act of independence that gives one the character to walk one's own road. Until this encounter is completed, one must rely on the strength of others to survive life's tragedies. Although the guidance and support of others is an integral part of human development, when you face your dragons, you will face them alone. Community may help you prepare for and recover from the encounter but at the heart of every encounter with your dragon, you will be alone.

People who refuse to deal with their dragons live with a pseudo identity crisis. The identity crisis is not genuine because they *do* know what they need to do with their lives — they know very well. But since they will not face adversity, they never become the person they must be to fulfill their mission. The dragon can bring many questions but it also conveys a clear direction. When it asks, "What will you do with me?", it is also saying: "You must deal with me!"

People who never move beyond their dragons may know what they are but they never know what they *could* be. They never know what they *should* be. They never come to be what they are meant to be. This is not a genuine identity crisis. Once you feel your yearning, your identity has begun to emerge. Your direction becomes apparent although your destination may not. People who decide not to face their dragons may call their condition an identity crisis (or others may label it an identity crisis for them), but this situation would be more accurately described as a crisis of courage.

Adversity always asks the question, "What will you do with me?" In order to deal successfully with adversity you must do three things. First, you must look your dragon in the eye. Next, you will need a skill or a weapon to protect yourself. Often the dragon will be invulnerable to techniques you have used in the past so you must now learn the skill(s) needed to assert yourself against this creature. Third, you need to respect the dragon. If you do not it may destroy you.

When you walk toward your adversity, you get a glimpse at what lies beyond it. It may seem as if your monster is teasing you by showing you something you can never have. In truth, this glimpse is to help you generate the courage to transcend your adversity. We see all that life could be if we are willing to risk in order to get there. This willingness to risk is not the *result* of courage; it *is* courage. When someone says, "I don't have enough courage," they are really saying, "I'm not willing to risk. Not even for a cause I know is meant for me." Everyone who travels this far encounters a dragon. Not everyone risks challenging it.

Like fear, all dragons have their lessons. While they are capable of destroying you, they are also capable of teaching you. Usually, the lesson does not become visible until you have survived the adversity. Consider, for instance, the most difficult teacher you ever encountered while in school. How did you survive? What did you learn? You may not have received any medals for this ordeal but that doesn't matter. You are better for your scars. Isn't it interesting that so many people identify their toughest teacher as their best teacher? It's worth noting, though, that the value of the teacher may not have been realized until after, sometimes long after, you moved on. It's not unusual for the lessons of the dragon to take root after the fact.

By the way, you may have also learned that those scars that were inflicted upon you have turned to seeds. Some seeds grow faster than others. Still, your scars can become your stars. They can produce your most heavenly and spiritual qualities.

When you are wounded by adversity, you are humbled. Some people refuse to accept being humbled and build as many lies as needed to hide the scars. They may compensate for their wounds by appearing grandiose and invulnerable. Their image belies the hurt within. A person who refuses to be humbled must live a lie. Beyond this, a person who does not accept his scars will never become truly empowered. Scars become the seeds of power.

Your limitations point you toward your strengths. When you accept your flaws, you accept all of you. You may begin your encounter with your dragon with an inflated ego, but you will not survive with one. Dragons seem to target the ego. It's as if its purpose is to attack the ego. The lesson here is that conceit and excessive pride are no longer allowed. If you hope to move past the dragon, you must leave them behind.

This is the paradox of the dragon. Conquering and sur-

viving your adversity can empower you. It can build the kind
of self-confidence that prepares you for the rest of your journey. Yet, at the same time, it is a deeply humbling experience.
All dragons leave wounds. An encounter with the dragon leaves
us humbled and empowered. Sooner or later, one who has conquered a dragon comes to understand that genuine personal
empowerment is ultimately linked to humility. Empowerment
keeps one's head up and one's eyes looking boldly toward the
past, present, and future. Humility keeps one's feet on the
ground. Until one's feet touch the ground, the journey cannot continue.

There may, of course, be more than one dragon in your
life. Each presenting its own challenge. Each requiring you to
risk. Each with its own lesson. If you refuse to face your dragons, your life will be an endless parade of these creatures. Even
the small things will become dragons. But conquering a dragon
will not rid them from your life altogether either. It's just that
until you conquer that first dragon, you will not have the qualities needed to move along on the road to you. A successful
encounter with a dragon will leave you empowered and
humbled. With these, you are prepared to move on.

As you go, there may be other dragons. They may appear
merciless and they may come at times when you are particularly vulnerable. But, for the most part, once you have been
empowered and humbled, you will have become a stronger and
wiser warrior. You will be better prepared for whatever adversity may lie ahead.

WOUNDEDNESS

If you choose to deal with your dragons, you will be wounded.
Yet from these wounds come wisdom, strength, and humility.
There are, however, two more possible consequences of being

wounded, both of which are essential to human growth. When one is wounded, one may (1) lose one's false self, and (2) learn about pain and healing.

Adversity has a way of exposing you. Not in a shaming way, but in a way that presents you in a most genuine, human light. Tragedy zaps the energy that you needed to build and maintain your pretenses. Adversity also affects your memory a little. You forget why you ever thought it was important to be pretentious anyway. Priorities change. Or, more accurately, you are reminded of what your real priorities have always been. You get reacquainted with the priorities beneath the pretense.

People who have survived a dragon with honor have a way about them. Maybe the dragon cracked the shell or ripped the hide off, but they understand that all that perished was their false self. Their arrogance and unhealthy pride crumbled and left them with their honest, genuine self. In order to survive with honor, the honesty and genuineness must remain. Should the pretense reemerge, then one has not survived the dragon with honor.

The dragon is an essential feature of the road to you because it is capable of destroying the false self. Some people are so caught up in their false self that — when it is destroyed — they feel they have been completely destroyed. For some this is a self-fulfilling prophecy and they destroy themselves during the course of or in the wake of adversity. The healthier response is to recognize that what has been exposed is the real self. The real self may be far from complete and it may be far from perfect, but it's the genuine you.

This exposure of the real self is a part of being humbled. If one has the willingness to accept one's real self as it emerges from the encounter with adversity, one becomes capable of developing much deeper, more honest interpersonal relationships. We recognize genuineness in others. It's as if we have a natural inclination to appreciate what's real.

One of the finest little stories I have ever come across that demonstrates how we appreciate honesty and authenticity in others was written by John Robert Clarke in his book, *The Importance of Being Imperfect.* According to Clarke's tale, there once lived a king who desired the hand of a visiting princess. In order to win her, he told her: "I am the Emperor of all Christendom." But she was not impressed, nor did she move toward him with love. He came closer then, and said: "Thousands of people move at my bidding." And still her smile did not inflame his hopes. With exasperation, leaning above her he cried: "Kings and emperors envy me my throne! Does this not move thee?" And she remained unmoved, nor did she smile upon him.

Now he languished. Sinking into his throne with weariness he said: "This is the way with me these days. You know, I did a bunch of stupid things even from this throne today; and, besides, my feet hurt." Slowly her smile fell upon him, warm and loving.[1]

Wounds, be they sore spirits or sore feet, are among the most recognizable signs of our vulnerability and, thus, our humanity. If we are willing to share these pains, we present ourselves as humbled (i.e., real) human beings. This does not mean that we are without power; it means that we have the courage and the willingness to be genuine. Not only does this make us more approachable and likeable to others, it really makes us more likeable to ourselves. Both are important because in order to reach your destination on the road to you, you will have to be comfortable with other people and yourself.

Although it may not seem possible at the time of the injury, wounds heal. Scars may remain but healing occurs nonetheless. Healing is the most miraculous event that most of us experience in our lifetimes. Healing grows out of woundedness. Again we see the connection between power and humility.

Healing teaches us hope. Hope is the light at the end of the tunnel, the star at the end of the journey. It is faith in what could be. The body, mind, and spirit all have the capacity to heal. So often, hope is faith in our ability to heal.

To those who have lost faith in their ability to mend, life becomes terrifying. Without this faith, they feel they could be destroyed at any time. They have no confidence that they can get up if they are knocked down. Just as troubling is the fact that when someone loses faith in their ability to heal, they lose their willingness to risk. And without risk, there can be no commitment.

Sometimes people have to be wounded before they develop a faith in healing. (Unfortunately, certain people have to be injured over and over before they accept the power of healing.) If the wound does not kill you it can indeed make you stronger.

As wounds heal and a faith in the process builds, so too does hope. A person who knows she can heal can accomplish so much more than one who lacks this confidence. The person who believes in healing can look to the future hopefully. She begins to feel that she has a destination. She now has a reason to survive adversity. With a destination — a reason to travel through the dragons — this soul is more likely to take risks in the effort to follow her yearning. As she takes these risks, she becomes more connected with her journey. With each risk it becomes less likely that she will turn and run from a dragon or her destination.

As the determination to stay the course builds, so does one's ability to conquer future dragons. With the lessons learned from past dragons, one becomes better prepared to deal with other forms of adversity that may develop down the line. Every form of adversity prepares you for the life you have ahead of you. More specifically, with each dragon you face with honor, you become more loyal to your journey.

With each successful encounter, you become better at naming your dragons. Once named, you see your adversity for what it really is. Then you know what you are dealing with. Having accomplished this you can address your monsters and even, sometimes, dialogue with them. The encounter with the dragon is much more than a meeting of two forces bent on destroying each other. Although destruction is possible, it is not inevitable, nor is it always desirable. Sometimes you will need to fight. But you will always need to think. Only by thinking, will you be able to answer your dragon when it asks, "What will you do with me?"

IMAGINARY DRAGONS

Not all dragons are real. Many people have a knack for creating mirages that appear as adversity. You could argue that if someone believes in imaginary dragons enough, then they become just as dangerous as the real ones. Well, there's some truth to this. But the wounds received in an encounter with an imaginary dragon are self-inflicted. You wound yourself. The most important lesson you can learn in this situation is exactly this: that you are hurting yourself. Unlike an encounter with a real dragon, you don't learn much from a self-inflicted wound. Hopefully, you will learn to stop and then get on with your life. But you don't really begin to learn until you get on with your life.

I once heard it referred to as the fight you can never win — the fight against yourself. You never really get past an imaginary dragon. That would require getting past yourself. You deal with imaginary dragons by understanding that they are imaginary. They disappear when you change your thinking. Then you move on.

Imaginary dragons neither humble nor empower you.

They only slow you down. We may all have them at one time or another so it is important that we see them for what they are. They vanish when we correct our thinking. They don't ask anything of us because they have no voice of their own. Their only substance is our biases and our dysfunctional thinking.

To help demonstrate how an imaginary dragon might present itself, I will describe a few of them here. These are only a sample of the unlimited number of imaginary monsters that we can conjure up.

The "What Ifs." — Here a person prepares for every form of disaster that could possibly arise. These potential catastrophes can range from the somewhat reasonable (e.g., What if I get cancer?) to the absurd (e.g., What if a meteor lands on me while I'm driving?). The individual who invents imaginary dragons out of "what ifs" is limited only by his or her imagination. A what-iffer can make his world a terrifying place. It is important to remember, however, that he is not so much the victim of the terror as he is the creator. You wouldn't help him much by teaching him how to live with his terror. Real healing begins when he accepts that he is creating his own terror. Once he takes responsibility for terrorizing himself, he can decide whether or not he wants to continue.

"Rejection will kill me." — This is a favorite. Like most destructive beliefs, there is an element of "what if" to it. People who believe that rejection is powerful enough to destroy them, tend to prepare for it constantly. And while they are insulating themselves from the pain of the inevitable rejections that are lurking everywhere, they retreat rather than grow. It's not that they "go it alone." They don't go at all. Because they imagine rejection is so overpowering, their defense is to avoid situations that could produce it. Ergo, they avoid human contact.

When intimacy is blocked by this imaginary dragon, a would-be traveler is left alone, without guidance or direction.

"I need to be perfect." — Ah, the imaginary dragon sometimes called perfectionism. People who fight this creature only feel successful when they perform at the 100% level. 99% means failure. To live with this standard they must limit their worlds to events that have a minimal potential for failure. If they don't meet their self-imposed standards, they not only experience failure, they feel they themselves have become failures. In other words, when they fall short of the imaginary dragon's demands, the dragon (they believe) swallows them.

Some people mature out of this. Since failure is an almost inevitable part of life, even the most cautious perfectionist is exposed to it. While the expectation of disaster can be a self-fulfilling prophecy, I like to think that most people eventually see that the sky doesn't fall and the earth doesn't crumble when they get a B+. Some learn faster than others that this monster has no substance. Like all imaginary dragons, when you realize that it is not real, it disappears.

"I'm not good enough." — People who live being trampled by this imaginary beast make decisions about themselves without looking fairly at the evidence. The juries in their heads are hanging juries. They like to convict.

These people never give themselves a fair trial. They're sure they are guilty even before opening arguments are made. They are usually not sure why they are so inadequate. It's just something they have to live with. It's as if some fire breathing monster's relentless attacks are keeping them from becoming good enough.

Some people, especially children, have reason to doubt their adequacy. If they are told often enough by people who are significant to them that they are inadequate, they tend to believe it. It can be hard to rise above this discouragement. Yet many do. The key is to recognize that your inadequacy is imaginary. Shame is a lie. Anyone who led you to believe that you are inherently inadequate was wrong.

When you recognize that you are fighting a mirage, your life becomes more sane and productive. All that time, energy, and attention you spent combating an illusion can now be used in the service of health. Again, to get to this point you don't have to kill anything. You have to separate what's real from what's not real. Although it can take some time to accept that what you have been struggling with for so long doesn't exist, it's more than worth the effort. Imaginary enemies can lead to devastating, even fatal, self-inflicted wounds.

"The world is dangerous." — Goethe once wrote, "We see what we know." He knew that we tend to see what we believe. If we believe that the world is a dangerous place, we will see danger everywhere. What's worse, this imaginary dragon blocks our view of all the wonderful qualities that exist in our world. We won't see the kindness, caring, and love. We just see the horrible things that could happen at any moment.

This belief can be difficult to dispel because there is an element of truth to it. There *is* danger in our world. In fact, there is enough of it that we can focus exclusively on the evil and use it to support our contention that evil is everywhere. Maybe we have cause to build this imaginary dragon. But the evil that exists is not large enough to obscure the resilient beauty and goodness that surrounds us. In reality, the dragon is not nearly that big. When we see through the imaginary, we encounter a world filled with more beauty and goodness than we could possibly see in a lifetime.

Other imaginary dragons are made up of such erroneous beliefs as, "*Everyone* must approve of everything I do," "You can't trust people," and "Only weak people show their feelings." These notions create obstacles that keep people stuck. They can destroy a person who believes them.

These beliefs are not real dragons because they exist only in the mind. Real dragons are those external crises that are sent by a force other than ourselves. These are the illnesses, injuries, failures, and losses that enter our lives and threaten our dreams. No matter how clearly and accurately you think, these dragons still arise. They are life's tragedies, and if you seek to live a full life, they will be a part of your story.

If you remove the imaginary dragons from your life, you will have more energy, cunning, perseverance, and courage to deal with the real ones.

CONCLUSION

The dragons in your life can chase you from your potential. They can devastate your spirit. Your dragons can keep you stuck, frustrated, and bitter. Your road may include more pain and heartache than you ever expected.

The danger is real.

But the danger is necessary. The road to you requires qualities that are developed through the encounter with adversity. The dragon strips away the false self, leaving one unpretentious and more real. This awakening makes you more real to yourself and to others. It represents another step forward in getting to know and expressing the real you.

One could certainly shed the false self and then recover it later. With each dragon you deal with successfully, however, this becomes less likely. Every time you face your dragon you take a risk. It is through these risks that you commit yourself to becoming who you are meant to be. As this commitment deepens, the need and desire to retreat dwindles.

A successful encounter with adversity means that you face your dragon with honor. This means you hold firmly to your honesty and integrity even when it appears that your life would be a lot easier if you took a less-than-honest shortcut or two.

As an example of this, consider the story of Carolyn. Carolyn was a psychology graduate student at a large university. She was in the final leg of her five year odyssey to achieve her doctoral degree when she came upon her doctoral exams. She had always been a determined student who worked hard for her good grades. She had completed everything that was asked of her; still, she became terrified of the doctoral exams.

Carolyn knew for some time that part of her calling was to be a psychologist. She felt the yearning and decided to move with it. But she knew that standing between her and her entrance into the professional world stood that dragon — the doctoral exams.

Carolyn sat for those eight hours of testing and passed just as everyone expected she would. Her life seemed to be unfolding as any story would that ended with "happily ever after." Then came the surprise. Carolyn had passed the test, but not the dragon. She had cheated. Because she had cheated she did not pass the dragon with honor. In so doing, the dragon moved out of her path and into her soul. Now it was part of her. She could not run from the problem; the creature was inside her, wreaking torment.

Now faced with a much larger dragon, she chose to look this one in the eye and put herself back on her path. Although no one suspected her of any wrongdoing, Carolyn confessed to the university. The dragon left her soul. Her situation, though, was one that circulates quickly through institutions of higher education. Her reputation was ravaged. She also received a series of sanctions for her crime. But, largely because she brought forth her own dishonesty, she was eventually allowed to take the test again. This time she was not nearly as afraid.

She passed the exam and moved on — humbled, wounded, and empowered.

If you deal with your dragons in an honorable way, they will make you stronger. Conquering serious adversity leaves you wounded and triumphant. The enemy becomes the teacher. You become better prepared to discover yourself and fulfill your mission because an honest encounter with the dragon leaves you humbled and empowered.

The wounds left by adversity may never heal completely. Still, to the extent that they do, they put you in touch with the miracle of healing. Belief in the human capacity to heal is, for most people, the first big step in the development of faith. When you heal you see evidence of a power that is real although perhaps not yet completely comprehensible. Experiencing healing also instills hope. You learn that in spite of all the tragedy in the world, much can be mended.

An honest encounter with the dragon leaves you humbled and empowered. After such an experience you are humbled and more real. You will have learned to hope. The fear you felt in the face of adversity and the healing you experienced after being wounded may have ignited a faith in a Higher Power or it may have deepened the faith you already owned. In all, you emerge from this phase of your journey changed and yet closer to your genuine self than you have ever been.

Having survived and learned from the dragon, one must now deal with the frightening forces from within.

CHAPTER FOUR

THE SHADOW

Years ago, Carl Jung identified a crucial dimension of the human psyche that he called the shadow. The shadow is the realm of our being where we place the negative and unwanted parts of ourselves. It contains the disliked characteristics that one is unwilling to recognize.

According to Jungian therapist Michael Daniels, the shadow houses the "dark or hidden side of a person's nature." It "represents our dark, hidden, repressed nature. It is the side of our character that we reject or deny because it conflicts with our conscious tendencies or our opinions about the self."[1] It's those pieces of ourselves that we don't want to believe.

The existence of the shadow explains why we resist honest self-examination. If you look deep enough inside yourself, you may run into things that upset or disgust you. Once these qualities are realized, and thus brought into consciousness, a person's identity changes. Accommodation must be made to deal with this material. Returning this information to the depths of the unconscious is possible but comes at a price. To keep it there, one must never partake in honest self-searching. If one looks within, one could fall into the shadow.

And even if you could live without looking within, the material in the shadow may still rise to the surface. As I explained in Chapter One, repression requires mental energy. When one's mental energy is low, repressed material pushes its way into consciousness. With nothing to force its captivity in the basement, it rushes toward the light. The lock on the door to the shadow can be broken.

When this occurs the person experiences a painful — yet potentially therapeutic — crisis. Once the material in the shadow is made known, it can be worked through and integrated into one's identity. This produces a more honest, grounded personality. The person is humbled by recognizing his dark side and yet empowered as he comes to accept all of himself. He is also empowered because he no longer has to waste energy keeping the truth hidden away.

One especially intriguing fact about the shadow is that it may contain what most people would consider positive qualities and yet are thought of as unacceptable to a particular person. The individual, for instance, who has invested himself in developing an antisocial personality may be repulsed when he recognizes elements of compassion and nurturing within himself. He may have built an identity that puts his needs above all else and insists that the only real path in life is the short cut. Then come those moments when pieces of his shadow move into the light and he must confront his capacity for caring. Oddly enough, this can produce just as much of a crisis as when a compassionate person encounters his capacity for selfishness, cruelty, or violence.

Sometimes people place material in their shadow at one stage in life and try to deny it forever. Then, when they are older and this matter is no longer as offensive, they can have a tough time getting in touch with it. A common example of this is a man's desire and ability to nurture. A similar example might be a man's desire and ability to show feelings such as hurt and sorrow, feelings that our culture tends to consider feminine. Early in a man's life these qualities may be thought to be strictly taboo. Many men, particularly young men, feel that their nurturing, caring sides make them less than manly. So these wonderful characteristics are sentenced to the shadow.

But age has a way of enlightening us, and what was once unmasculine and dreadful begins to feel more welcome. The passage of time can correct some mistakes of youth, and young men who wouldn't allow themselves to care grow into warm-hearted gentlemen. The young father who would not permit himself to really get close to his children warms into a kind-hearted, affectionate grandfather. As he grew, he retrieved the gems he had abandoned while an insecure young man.

Then there is the more tragic story. Here the young man exiles his gentle, loving side into the dark reaches of the shadow but then, when he needs these qualities to help make life meaningful, he cannot reclaim them. He may feel the need for genuine intimacy but not be able to find the qualities he needs to reach this. And yet he may have a strange feeling that somewhere deep inside he has all that he needs to contribute to an intimate relationship.

While working in mental health and chemical dependency treatment programs over the years, I have heard countless men say, in one way or another, that they wished they could cry. They all know, of course, that they came into the world crying. And most of these men realize that they are responsible for ridding themselves of the option to cry. They just don't know where it went or how to get it back. But even though they speak of the desire to cry, most continue to fear it. They fear what is sometimes called the "affect storm"; that is, they fear that if they start to cry, they may never stop. They fear that if they start to cry for all the sadness they didn't cry for over the years, the tears may never end. Examining the shadow and bringing aspects of it into consciousness for the purpose of accepting it into your identity requires honesty, courage, and focus. To get enough courage and focus you may have to work through ambivalence. Integrating the shadow is difficult enough when you are ready. If you aren't sure, it's even harder.

This is one of the important differences between the dragons in your life and your shadow. The dragons (i.e., external adversity) are more likely to force themselves on you. Sometimes you can run away from them, but there are many dragons that block your escape. Dragons help you develop courage by forcing you into situations where you may not have other choices but to be courageous. This is why people typically encounter the dragon before the shadow. Until we have developed the character that comes with encountering the dragon with honor, we may not be ready to look at the adversity that lives within us.

Lots of people end their journeys here. Of those who successfully deal with the dragon, fewer successfully deal with the shadow. No one has to listen to the shadow. We have a choice. The yearning, however, is still there. It doesn't stop. The yearning is what drives us to look at the parts of ourselves that we would prefer to deny. At this point on the road to you, you are asked to stop hiding things from yourself. But the road has also prepared you for this. Conquering the dragon left you empowered and humbled (i.e., more willing to accept your flaws). The adversity you have survived may have also taught you the power of healing. When you believe in healing, you become less afraid.

People who never explore their shadows will continue to face dragons, both real and imaginary. This will produce a stream of sorrow and triumph that has its rewards, but eventually becomes frustrating. In the final analysis, the purpose of the dragon is to prepare you to move on. If you don't move on, you've never really survived it.

If you never examine your shadow, many of the dragons that come for you will be the imaginary kind. The material that a person keeps in the shadow tends to be projected on to other people. As Michael Daniels warns, "Often we project our shadow on to other people and see in them the qualities that we fail to recognize in ourselves. For this reason, whenever we show a strong irrational tendency to criticize or blame others, we should consider whether in fact the fault we are condemning is really our own."[2] Thus, someone who disowns feelings of aggressive ambition may wind up throwing this distaste on to others. If this projection goes on long enough, the person will begin to see the world as a place filled with cutthroats who care only about getting ahead. In other words, he or she will come to feel surrounded by dragons.

This projection continues until the material in the shadow is accepted and integrated into one's awareness and identity. In so doing, a person owns these qualities as their own and no longer tries to unload them on others.

We will deal more with the issue of integrating the shadow shortly. Before doing so, however, we need to consider the darker side of our callings. The lives we are called to are not without pain. Just as people misunderstand themselves because they refuse to accept their darker side, many people miss their callings because they refuse to respect its shadow.

THE SHADOW SIDE OF A CALLING

The life you are called to is not a perfect one. It will have its wonderful times and perfect moments, but it will also have its anguish. The yearning you feel will not take you to Camelot. If you wait for a path without pain, you will wait forever.

There are negative experiences that all callings seem to share and then there are unique hurts to each person's mission. First, let's consider the shadow side of all callings. Keep in mind, though, that the material kept in the shadow can be integrated into one's consciousness at any time. So while there are qualities that tend to dwell in the shadow, in individual cases they may have already been freed.

All callings ask you to accomplish something. Consequently, those who live their callings live with the threat of failure. Because they have already come this far, they have already demonstrated a willingness to risk. Still, failure — especially in endeavors as important as one's calling — hurts. People who seek to accomplish live with failure. It's part of their lives, a painful part. I can't prove it, but I'm prepared to believe that everyone who lives his or her calling fails at one point or another. I also believe that most people know this at the time they accept their callings.

Being aware of the possibility of failure can make us more effective in the work we do. It can keep us focused and can produce a level of anxiety that enhances performance. If we bring the fear of failure into our awareness, it can be motivating. This is an example of how the shadow can benefit us if we accept it and integrate it into our lives.

Callings are not pain free. Besides the failure, there is the loss of freedom. When you choose one path, you forsake many others. You may have been successful in those other efforts. Those memories of success don't go away easily. Whenever you hit a rough patch of road, those memories have a way of kicking in. They remind you of how much easier it could have been if you had taken a different path.

Along with the loss of freedom there is also frustration. This isn't the easy way. Not only will there be frustration, much of the frustration you will have to deal with alone.

Being alone with frustration and failure can lead to doubt. Everyone's road has doubt. Sometimes we deny it because of the anxiety it generates. When the thought, "Maybe I'm not where I should be," arises, it produces fears of having to start all over again someplace else. Avoiding the discomfort means denying the doubt.

If we can accept the doubt and bring it into our consciousness, we find that this too has its rewards. It forces a reexamination of who we are and where we are going. This soul searching can leave one rejuvenated with a new enthusiasm for what one is becoming. Working through doubt, like working through all material in the shadow, can make you a happier, healthier person. But you don't find the happy ending until you work through the junk.

No calling is painless. Besides the dark side that seems to be a part of all callings, there is a shadow side to specific callings. Healers are in constant contact with suffering. Leaders live with criticism. Those who are called to create, face the torment of living through times when their creativity is gone. Educators know that not all of their students are eager to learn. Those who dedicate themselves to the fight for justice, perhaps more than anyone else, see the most vulgar injustices.

People who integrate the shadow side of their callings live with a far greater awareness of where they are and what needs to be done. But, again, this awareness comes with a price. One must look at the immensity of the task at hand. Once we look at this, we tend to either grow or shrink.

WORKING THROUGH

Some time ago I had a difficult conversation with a fifty-five-year-old woman. Two days prior to this meeting, her daughter had been brutally raped by two strangers. Her daughter survived but the extent of the damage was still anything but clear. She had been severely cut on the face and arms. This mother raised the fear of AIDS but couldn't say this in anything louder than a whisper. Because her daughter had spoken very little since the attack, many of the details of the awful incident remained unknown. This mother was left with her fear and imagination to fill in the blanks.

As this mother spoke, her anger became more and more visible. At the point when it appeared that she was about to launch into a rage, she cried, "I'm a Christian woman! I shouldn't feel this way! I just want to... I just want to..." She couldn't bring herself to say it. At least not to me.

This woman was confronted by two powerful crises, one leading to the other. First came the horrible assault on her daughter. This then led to a second crisis. She had not been aware of her capacity for rage and contempt. Nor was she aware of her potential for cruelty. She wanted these men to feel pain. But this desire was not consistent with her view of what a "Christian woman" should be.

This woman was placed in a situation where she was forced to deal with some of the darkest material in her shadow. (In this case a dragon put her in touch with her shadow.) She had convinced herself that she was without this kind of venom. She didn't want to think of herself this way. But it was there all along.

I don't say any of this in a judgmental way. She had a right to every ounce of her anger. People don't put material into their shadow because it's necessarily evil. We put it there because it is a part of us that we don't feel we can live with. When we look into our shadows we see the greed, the rage, the competitiveness that we refuse to accept in ourselves.

Putting this material in the shadow makes it easier, at least in the short run, to be the person you want to be. Most of us, for instance, want to be strong and independent, so we throw our neediness into the dark side. We put it there with the hope that it will disappear.

In order to understand who we are, we must reclaim the parts of ourselves that we have tried to abandon. Without integrating all our pieces, we cannot be whole. But integrating the shadow is particularly difficult because it is the piece (or, actually pieces) of ourselves that we least want to accept. Indeed, it is the collection of traits that we would most like to destroy.

"One does not become enlightened by imagining figures

of light," wrote Jung, "but by making the darkness conscious." This does not mean that we should embrace or revel in the dark side of ourselves. Rather, we need to integrate all the realms of our beings. Because the shadow is the most difficult (i.e., painful) aspect of our psyches to bring into awareness, this is precisely the point where so many of us quit the path to enlightenment.

When we first become aware that the shadow exists and understand its purpose, we face alternatives. Author and psychiatrist Edward C. Whitmont summarizes the options:

> There are several kinds of reactions to the shadow. We can refuse to face it; or, once aware that it is part of us, we can try to eliminate it and set it straight immediately; we can refuse to accept responsibility for it and let it have its own way; or we can "suffer" it in a constructive manner, as a part of our personality which can lead us to a salutary humility and humanness and eventually to new insights and expanded life horizons.[3]

We can move from one response to another before settling with one. But until we face the shadow and bring it into the light, we live with the unsettledness that comes with running from who we are. Benjamin Franklin once said, "Those things that hurt, instruct." We don't mind bringing forth our talents and strengths. It's our flaws we deny.

Other than this, tapping the shadow is not a terribly difficult process. There are no locks on it. It's not booby trapped, nor is it surrounded by demons. If it goes untouched, it is only because the person does not want to touch it.

Not only is it relatively easy to examine your shadow, it is easier to examine it than it is to avoid it. Certainly, becoming aware of your dark side takes determination and courage. We prefer not to have deficiencies, and opening the shadow means looking right at our flaws. But as challenging as this can be, it is much more difficult to live our lives avoiding our dark side. The material we stuff into the shadow does not rest peacefully. In fact, it does not rest at all. It moans and groans and reaches and grows. It fights the denial that tries to banish it from awareness. This fight sends tremors through one's entire being.

It often makes its presence known in less than direct ways. As mentioned previously, one of the most common ways the shadow asserts itself is through projection. Here an individual projects his shadow on to other people. Usually he is not aware of it. He throws his faults on to other people and thus he tends to see these defects in them. What he is really seeing, of course, are his own unacceptable qualities that he has tried to keep tucked away in his shadow. The flaws that we keep seeing over and over may actually be a part of us.

Jungian analyst William A. Miller explains an approach to identify one's projections and thus become aware of one's shadow:

> The simplest method is to list all of the qualities we do not like in other people; for instance, conceit, short temper, selfishness, bad manners, greed, and others. When the list is finally complete (and it will probably be quite lengthy), we must exact those characteristics that we not only dislike in others, but hate, loathe, and despise. This shorter final list will be a fairly accurate picture of our personal shadow. This will probably be very hard to believe and even harder to accept.[4]

Getting in touch with the parts of us that we feel are unacceptable is, in its own way, a form of suffering. It's looking in the mirror and seeing ugliness. It's looking into your heart and seeing greed. It's looking into your soul and feeling unworthy of a soul. Jung claimed that "neurosis is always a substitute for legitimate suffering." That is, we stunt our emotional and spiritual growth when we refuse to proceed when the road gets painful.

Examining the shadow can be extremely beneficial to our emotional and spiritual health. Knowing this, Jung once referred to the material in the shadow as "pure gold." We put material in our shadow to avoid the discomfort of growth. Consequently, the shadow is filled with the potential for growth. All those things that require you to stretch and reach farther than you thought possible are waiting for you there.

If you haven't worked through your fears, you've shoved them into your shadow. If you've decided your self-centeredness is unconquerable, you've plunged it into your dark side. And if your anger seemed so immense that you couldn't work with it, you forced it into the darkness within. Now, should you decide to continue on the road to you, you need to become acquainted with the dimensions of you that you have tried to hide in the darkness.

I must emphasize here that a person places material in his shadow that he feels is inconsistent with the idealized image he has of himself. A man, for example, who wants more than anything to be tough and macho, may exile his capacity for compassion and tenderness into his shadow. It's not that the material itself is bad, it's just that these characteristics do not help him become the man he thinks he needs to be. And so it is that even our healthiest traits can end up in the dungeon.

There is perhaps no more tragic an example of this than unaccepted spirituality. Our culture respects those who are self-reliant and independent. The desire for strength and control can put people in the center of their universe. They are comfortable with people needing them. But they're not so accepting of their need for anyone or anything else.

These souls delegate their spiritual dimension to the shadow for several reasons. First, they believe that the existence of a Higher Power will make them appear smaller. It's not that they necessarily deny the existence of God — it's just that they tend not to pay much attention to Him. Second, for a self-absorbed individual, the spiritual world is a distraction. It's something that he promises himself he will concern himself with later. Right now, he's focused on things that affect his image. Third (and this ties into the first two), spirituality has a way of humbling us. The universe gets much larger when we open the door to the spiritual realm. A whole new set of unanswered question presents itself. One's certainty becomes a little less certain. Finally, to some folks, spirituality is weakness. They see it as a crutch that other people use when they can't handle their problems. Even though the spiritual dimension is a part of everyone, if it's thought to be inconsistent with the person one wants to be, there is a good chance that it will be buried in one's dark side.

This explains why there is often such a strong spiritual component to the process of connecting with the shadow. All the spirituality that was hidden away moves into awareness. With it comes new questions, concerns, and priorities. When one's spirituality emerges one becomes humbled and empowered, the two qualities that are a part of all growth.

When the shadow moves into the light, we move closer to enlightenment. Out of the darkness come the missing pieces that complete us. Mythologist Joseph Campbell described this well: "One thing that comes out of myths is that at the bottom of the abyss comes the voice of salvation. The black moment is the moment when the real message of transformation is going to come. At the darkest moment comes the light."

In order to feel the warmth of the light we must face the fear of the darkness. The shadow can reveal itself in our dreams, our projections, and our moments of honest, courageous reflection. Keep in mind that the shadow is a place where we try to keep things. It does not have real power of its own. We don't have to negotiate with it. We control it. It comes into awareness when we want it to. The shadow is not a particularly effective jail. The material it tries to contain is always escaping.

Pieces of the dark side force their way to the surface causing unexplainable outbursts of jealousy, bitterness, or egotism. The shadow is far from escape proof. Until we open the shadow and accept as our own what we have stored in it, these eruptions will continue. Material that needs to be dealt with picks its moments to make itself heard. These moments are unpredictable and can wreak havoc on a person's life. But when the shadow material is deliberately brought into awareness, the surprise attacks stop. Life becomes less chaotic.

When we decide to confront the shadow, we can be somewhat overwhelmed by what we are presented with. It may be helpful to have someone to help process and sort it out. Sometimes a professional counselor can assist with this. Another person can help point things out that might otherwise be missed. Also, the support and encouragement that one person can give another can aid the process. When someone examines the characteristics that she tried to hide, it can be good to hear someone else say, "You're still O.K."

How you throw light on your shadow is as unique as you are. There is one method, though, that I have seen work with a number of people. This technique is usually called "sentence stems" and it involves completing sentences, such as the following, as many ways as you can.

1. I have trouble living with the fact that I....

2. People might not accept/like/love me if they knew that I....

3. The thing that bothers me most about people is....

4. I have never told anyone that I....

5. I've never believed it, but I've been told that I....

How you finish these sentences can help you identify the contents of your shadow by pointing to (a) the qualities you already know you are trying to hide (i.e., sentences 1 and 2), (b) elements of your shadow that you may be projecting on to others (i.e., sentence 3), and (c) material in your shadow that others may see more clearly than you do (i.e., sentences 4 and 5).

If you decide to examine your shadow, for a time your dreams may change. Whenever material from the unconscious is released, dreams are affected. The change may be pleasant or unpleasant. When shadow material enters consciousness via dreams, these dreams may be upsetting. Not necessarily nightmares, these dreams place one in a position where one is surrounded by the things he once tried so hard to repress. The middle-aged male workaholic dreams of himself strolling through a garden with small children. This dream could be a sign that he is bringing his nurturing side into the light. The introverted woman dreams of herself leading troops into battle. This might indicate that she is becoming acquainted with her aggressive or, perhaps, heroic qualities. Such dreams may create more curiosity or wonder than they do fear. At the time in life that a person examines his shadow, the material here may not be as appalling as when he first put it away. The man mentioned above may now be ready to go to the garden. The woman may be willing to go to battle.

But there is always the chance that what you pull from your shadow may still be difficult to accept. You may find sensitivity, tenacity, self-centeredness, or compulsivity. And the ending here isn't always a completely happy one. Those qualities which are part of you that you cannot accept may never change or go away. They may be traits you will have to learn to live with.

A common example of this is sensitivity. Many people — men and women — don't want to deal with this side of themselves. While sensitivity can serve you well in interpersonal relationships and help you become more creative, sensitivity can make you vulnerable. Sensitive people are easily wounded. They are injured by the slights and insensitivities of others. These hurts can take time to heal; some never seem to repair. Remaining vulnerable can lead to more hurt. Albert Schweitzer said there is a "fellowship of those who bear the mark of pain." Feeling pain can connect one with humanity. But it still hurts.

People have gone to great lengths to rid themselves of their sensitivity. They jade themselves with layers and layers of an "I don't care" attitude. Many convince themselves that their sensitivity is really depression and then enlist others to help them squelch it. What's worse, there are well-intentioned psychotherapists who collude with this destructive practice. These misguided professionals believe that if something hurts, it must be unhealthy.

Hurt can be a sign of health. Sensitivity can hurt; healing often does. There doesn't seem to be a way to change this. When you accept your sensitivity, it will still lead to heartache sometimes. Taking ownership of your sensitivity won't make the bruises go away. When you release it from your shadow, you take the pain that comes with it.

No, becoming aware of what is in your shadow won't make you perfect. In fact, it usually increases your awareness of your imperfection. Becoming aware of your imperfection, though, may be the greatest reward for exposing your shadow. Only a person who is willing to have flaws can truly know himself. Only then can he maintain his honesty. A person who only knows his strengths, doesn't know himself.

Then too, a person who knows only his powers may not be capable of intimacy. This soul wouldn't have a lot to share. Disclosing one's strengths soon becomes shallow. Revealing one's hurts, doubts, and confusion communicates a vulnerability that creates trust. This trust will be essential in the next stage of the road to you. Once someone has begun to shine the light on their shadow, he is ready to move on. The next stage involves building healthy relationships. After you have integrated your shadow, you have enough self-awareness to (1) find the people who are right for you, and (2) present yourself honestly.

Uncovering the shadow is, as much as anything, an ordeal of honesty. The shadow doesn't lie. It is the ego that is capable of lying. The ego will deny, distort, repress — all in an effort to avoid that which makes it uncomfortable. The shadow, on the other hand, doesn't do any of these. The shadow houses what the ego denies.

No one begins to uncover the shadow until they possess a desire for honesty. You are ready to know your shadow when you are ready to know who you are. You are ready to know your shadow when you are prepared to be honest with yourself.

No one ever comes to know themselves without this honesty. At this point in the journey, honesty is the most important quality you can own. The encounter with the shadow starts with a desire for honesty. As the material in the shadow is brought into awareness, honesty grows. First, a person is more honest with himself. He is now looking at the parts of himself that he once denied. He has stopped lying to himself.

Once someone becomes more honest with himself, it is inevitable that he will be more honest with others. If you are not ashamed of yourself, you will have no shame to project on to others. When you accept yourself, you find more people who are accepting of you.

When you are honest with yourself you are better able to see people as they are. You no longer need others to help you deny what you don't want to see in yourself. Your relationships become more genuine and spontaneous because you no longer fear exposure. This is the feeling: "Sure I have flaws but I'm still O.K." Or maybe Marty, from the 1955 film by the same name, said it best when he remarked that "dogs like us, we ain't such dogs as we think we are."

Honesty, if we maintain it, takes us to forgiveness. When people say "I can't forgive myself," it's usually because they haven't been honest enough. They're still hiding things. We are not capable of forgiving ourselves for hidden offenses. Nothing can be forgiven until it is revealed. Honesty precedes forgiveness.

Not only does honesty lead to forgiveness, it also opens the door to all kinds of healing. Honesty, for instance, has probably healed more broken relationships than all the marriage counselors in the world. It has also healed innumerable broken minds and deflated spirits. Honesty puts you in touch with you. It doesn't care about what someone else might want you to be; it only cares about who you really are. Honesty, if you stay with it, will always lead you back to you.

Without this honesty your path will be blocked. Honesty is essential for self-awareness. Healthy people are always in the process of growing. Self-awareness is an ongoing process. There will come a time however when your identity is essentially intact. At this point (which is the destination on the road to you), you need not focus on who you are but rather on what you need to do. Once one's identity is formed, one focuses more on one's mission.

Dealing with our shadow teaches us about honesty. Without this lesson we can go no further. Sadly, lots of people stop here. They can stare down a dragon, but they cannot face themselves.

But those who do are better for it. They no longer waste their energy hiding things. They take ownership of all their dimensions and accept the flaws that they cannot change. In this process a person often retrieves memories that were once too painful to keep in awareness. Once found, these memories contribute to one's identity. And because this person has been empowered by knowing that he has faced both the dragon and the shadow, difficult memories are now much less likely to make him feel like a victim. Instead, he feels like a survivor. Not necessarily in the triumphant or exultant sense but, rather, in a humbled and empowered way.

The well-known Serenity Prayer has provided guidance for millions of people. It reads:

> God grant me the serenity
> To accept the things I cannot change;
> Courage to change the things I can;
> And wisdom to know the difference.

This prayer speaks directly to those on the verge of looking into their shadow. You grow when you make constructive changes in your life. You also grow when you accept the parts of you that you cannot change. Even the imperfect parts.

CONCLUSION

Dealing with your shadow is an exercise in honesty. Without honesty you cannot continue on the road to you. Human beings have an astounding capacity for deceit. We are so good at this that we can fool ourselves for our entire lives.

When we are dishonest with ourselves, we don't make our bad things go away. Instead, they are sentenced to dwell in the shadow. The more we put in our shadow, the more unwanted, unintegrated baggage we have to carry around.

Robert Bly describes the shadow as "the long bag we drag behind us." As we put more and more material in our "bag" it grows and becomes heavier and harder to drag behind us.[5] Our challenge is to open our bag and empty it in a well-lit area. Then we can examine and integrate the material into our lives. This examination and integration does not magically correct all of our flaws. Being aware of how we are flawed, however, and accepting this, makes us more aware of who we are.

In their book *Meeting the Shadow*, Connie Zweig and Jeremiah Abrams describe the benefits of uncovering the shadow. Through an honest encounter with the shadow, we can

— achieve a more genuine self-acceptance, based on a more complete knowledge of who we are;
— defuse the negative emotions that erupt unexpectedly in our daily lives;
— feel more free of the guilt and shame associated with our negative feelings and actions;
— recognize the projections that color our opinions of others;
— heal our relationships through more honest self-examination and direct communication.[6]

You will always have a shadow. There will be times throughout your life when you will be tempted to hide parts of yourself there. Just as there will be dragons all along your path, so too there will be the shadow. Should you start to fill it again, it will drag you down and halt your journey. One unmistakable clue that your shadow is filling is the belief that you have no imperfections. When you start to believe that you have no faults or limitations, it's time to return to your shadow and begin again this ordeal of honesty.

Dealing with the shadow prepares you for honest and genuine interpersonal relationships. If you have maintained the honesty needed to see and accept what you have found, you are ready for intimacy.

It is at this point that you are prepared to know and appreciate your fellow travelers.

CHAPTER FIVE

FELLOW TRAVELERS

On the road to you there are times when you will be alone. During these periods you will know the solitude that produces stillness and insight. You will also experience the loneliness that leads to a hunger for human contact.

During the early stages on the road to finding ourselves, we spend quite a bit of time by ourselves. We hear a calling that no one else hears. We feel a yearning that no one else feels. In many of the struggles against our dragons, we fight alone. And most of the journey into our shadow is a solitary adventure. But now things change. Our next step involves leaving our aloneness. At this stage, one has enough of an identity to commit oneself to human relationships without being swallowed up.

Identity precedes intimacy. You must have an "I" before you can say "I do" or "I will". You have to have an identity before you can contribute to a relationship. One's identity, however, need not be complete or perfect. Intimacy will take an identity and nurture it and help it grow. If your roots are strong, your relationships will make you more aware of what you are meant to be. Identity leads to intimacy. But intimacy also enriches identity.

People who have survived dragons with their honor intact and brought light to their dark side will have much to bring to relationships. Although they (hopefully) have been in relationships since the day they were born, their relationships now have the potential to be much deeper and more mature. You have to begin to find yourself before you can give yourself. One who has successfully survived the dragon and the shadow has been humbled and empowered. She is aware that she has the strength and the character to weather hard times. She has learned about healing and forgiveness. Her scars help her empathize and her spirit gives her the vigor to support others. She is aware of her capacity for strength and weakness. Everything she has experienced has led her to an appreciation, respect, and love for humanity.

The cavemen came together and formed communities for the sake of protection. They formed survival relationships. While protection may still be the most basic need satisfied by communities, other essential needs are also involved. Human relationships fill emotional needs. We need to feel supported and appreciated by others. How we feel about ourselves is significantly affected by how other people act toward us. We need relationships to help us grow emotionally. These kinds of relationships are our emotional relationships.

Then there are the spiritual needs that are met through relationships. These relationships help you walk your path. They help you stay in touch with your yearning and they support you in your effort to follow it.

The deepest, most enduring relationships are those that have risen to the spiritual level. Here no one looks for personal rewards, even though the rewards are many. It is at this level that one comes to understand how giving is more important than receiving. Kahlil Gibran described this well in *The Prophet* when he wrote, "Let there be no purpose in friendship save the deepening of the spirit." You deepen the spirit through giving.

Someone who has followed his yearning through dragon and shadow has much to give. He has learned much. One must become an individual before one can truly join another individual or a community. This explains one of the most common causes of divorce. Marriages begin on shaky ground when the people involved have not developed enough of themselves. If they do not develop themselves, they will not have enough to share. They will not have enough to give. They will be unable to deepen the spirit.

Someone who has decided to follow his yearning and has traveled through his dragon and his shadow is pulled into relationships in much the same way he has been pulled toward his calling. The spirit has reasons that the mind and body do not know. This person feels pulled to unite with fellow travelers. The bond that grows feels healthy and natural. But perhaps the strongest indicator that this bond is an appropriate part of an individual's path is the energy that arises from the union. Good relationships produce energy, positive energy. We call this energy love or, sometimes, passion — and both terms are probably accurate. This can do more than make us feel good. It helps us become who we are meant to be.

Often the difference between a first grader who gets A's and one who gets D's is the fact that the A student has someone she loves who really appreciates the A's. She has someone to run home to who delights in what she has accomplished. Grades have no intrinsic value for small children. But if good grades makes someone they love happy, then they will constantly surpass themselves by improving their work. Because someone they love wants them to be the best they can be, they have the energy to do just that.

These are the relationships that bring out the best in you. The most fortunate among us have a number of these relationships. You may have this kind of relationship with your spouse or a friend, family member, teacher, employer, or coach. You don't have to wait for these relationships to come along. You can seek out the people whose love and friendship fuel your passion. Look for the people who produce energy in you. These are the souls who will help you become who you are meant to be.

So what does this say about relationships that lack energy? These, I'm afraid, may not be healthy relationships. At least not now. You see, there are different kinds of relationships with different kinds of energy problems. First, there are relationships that produce no energy at all. Sometimes these relationships can be repaired but it takes energy to do so. If the people are not willing to work toward improving this situation, the prognosis is poor.

Then there is the relationship that is filled with negative energy. This union is filled with conflict. Actually, this relationship may have a better chance of being repaired than the relationship that has no energy. Two people who are in a relationship filled with negative energy tend to make the same demand on each other. They both say, in one way or another, "I want you to stay with me but I want you to be different!" As they become aware of what they really want, they find they are really saying, "I want you to stay, but I want you to do things the way I think they should be done!"

Whenever one person communicates to another: "I will only accept you if you never change," that relationship has stopped being healthy. The cavemen may have only needed relationships for protection, but times have changed. Maybe in the caves we were purely physical beings, but we are now creatures with a very real and very strong spiritual dimension. We need our relationships to help us grow beyond security.

There may well be times in life when you will have to leave relationships because the energy has gone. Some of these relationships may have once been dear to you. Good-byes can be difficult. But sometimes they're necessary.

It's interesting, too, that some of these relationships come back later in life with a renewed energy. There are times, for instance, when young adults need to leave their parents for a while. All parties may grieve the loss of a bond that was to have lasted forever. Then, during the course of the grief and separation, something unpredictable occurs. It's as if once they have separated themselves into separate beings, they then find themselves back (or perhaps for the first time) in an energy-producing union.

Adults need their own boundaries and their integrity if they are to build the kind of relationships that deepen the spirit. Adults need relationships where growth is encouraged, and individuality is supported. In order to find such a relationship, you must become a person who can provide this kind of relationship for someone else. If you have not developed this in yourself, then what you are really looking for is an unhealthy parent. Someone who will take care of you without making any demands.

People who have spent time learning about and working to accept their shadow have more honest relationships because they have dropped their mask. They no longer need to carry the persona of perfection and invulnerability. They understand and accept that they are neither. They have come to learn of their flaws and limitations. As they accept the less-than-desirable qualities in themselves, they are more willing to share them with others. As they integrate their dark side, they become less pretentious. The mask falls away and is replaced with honesty.

People can usually sense this. We appreciate and admire those willing to admit the weaker side of themselves. Ironically, exposing your imperfection is often interpreted as a sign of strength. It is a sure indication of character when one's honesty is stronger than one's ego.

Surviving the dragon leaves one strong. Surviving the shadow leaves one honest. A person now has the qualities to build healthy relationships. When you are prepared to *contribute* to a healthy relationship, you are ready to find a healthy relationship.

ENCOURAGEMENT

The energy must continue. Surviving adversity produces energy. Bringing repressed material in the light also produces energy. But unless we want to live our lives dealing with crisis and turmoil, we need to find other sources of energy to fuel our journey in life. The yearning that began this passage is, of course, another potent source of energy. There will be times when this may be your only source. But we are far from perfect beings and we can, at times, lose touch with this source.

There are stretches when our spiritual condition becomes impacted by our psychological state. For example, when our spiritual energy runs low, so too does our mental energy. And when our psychological stamina dwindles, our spiritual vitality may be affected. When this situation occurs, at least three possible solutions present themselves. First, one could work to build the psychological energy. Second, one could move to rejuvenate the spirit. Or third — the preferred method — one might try to invigorate the mind and spirit together.

How is this done? One particularly powerful source of psycho-spiritual energy is encouragement. Encouragement, the process of giving courage or hope, vitalizes the psyche and the spirit. Receiving encouragement strengthens confidence and morale. It can boost psychological well-being. Encouragement is such a powerful and healthy force that Alfred Adler built his theories of education and psychotherapy around it. He argued against the use of the term "mental illness," insisting that more often than not people who are given this label are actually *discouraged*. The essence of psychotherapy, he claimed, is encouragement. When people are encouraged to be what they can be, they tend to become it.

There is also a second side to encouragement, the side that affects the spirit. Encouragement *received* nurtures our psychological side. Encouragement *given* empowers our spiritual being. We grow spiritually when we encourage someone else. Each time we give courage to someone, our spirit deepens. We become more connected with humanity and in the process we become more in touch with a larger spiritual force.

The feeling of connectedness is one of the best signs that the road we are following is the right one. This feeling of connectedness is, I suppose, a reward, but more than anything it is a sign. It's a sign that you are moving toward where you need to be.

How we benefit by receiving encouragement is an important topic. But it is not something I want to focus on here. If you would like to learn more about it, I recommend that you investigate Adlerian psychology, as much of this school of thought deals with the effects of receiving encouragement. Another way to learn how one is impacted by receiving encouragement is to experience it yourself. Look for someone who is skilled in and willing to give encouragement. Pay attention to what encouragement does to you.

What I want to consider here is the act of encouraging. This is the more spiritual side of the process. By encouraging others, we feel the connectedness that guides us. This connectedness can have an awesome power. Strangely, this power is intimidating to some. It's an experience so positively powerful that it moves people. The only way you will grow is if you allow yourself to be moved. But big growth experiences such as this, while very healthy, can be so powerful that they can make one feel a little out of control. It's this threat to one's sense of control that frightens people away.

Encouragement is such a powerful and sometimes frightening force that we have to create special opportunities for ourselves to practice it. Sports, for instance, serve this function. They allow us to scream our encouraging words with an intensity that feels completely natural. Most competitions for that matter, are opportunities to vent and control our need to encourage. Competition is never out of season. It's always there to meet the need.

But this is precisely the problem. It meets too much of the need. There's no question that athletics and many other forms of competition enrich our culture. When all, or most, of our energy for encouragement is invested in this one arena, however, our growth becomes stunted. When we spend our energies supporting teams of people we don't know and neglect the people beside us, our encouragement becomes shallow. We no longer feel the connectedness.

This is why so many in our culture have become "sports fanatics." They feel the inner need to encourage others, but they fear the intimacy. So they root for strangers and imagine a personal closeness that will never exist. This doesn't fill their hunger, so they eat more and more until the only things in their world that they are encouraging are "their teams." And the hunger continues.

There is a place for encouraging people from a distance. But you will never satisfy your need to encourage if you are only encouraging people from afar. We have a need to encourage people close to us. Encouragement is an important part of intimacy.

Good encouragers are always unique people. They stay true to themselves and are seldom shaped by criticism. Good encouragers are the best teachers, coaches, and managers you have ever seen. Often they are marvelous leaders, although some do their encouraging quietly, behind the scenes. They welcome, they receive, when they instill courage and drive in others. This energy is a focused energy that keeps them on task. They use this energy in pursuit of their own mission.

One of the best examples of the power of encouragement is to watch its effects on someone who has lost their energy. I know a retired teacher, for instance, who was not doing well in her retirement. Margaret had been a great teacher with a special talent for bringing out the best in "hard to reach" kids. She was an encourager. So energetic that some may have thought she was a little eccentric, she was in truth a very emotionally healthy person who always seemed to be fueled by love.

Everything went well for her until retirement. She then gradually lost her energy. She tried learning to paint and then sew but neither could sustain her interest. Her doctor feared she might be developing depression. She didn't know what to think.

Just as her situation began looking really bleak, fate stepped in. She had retired from teaching but she would always be a teacher. Margaret began to heal when a friend pointed her toward the Special Olympics. Before long she was volunteering at a number of child care facilities. Most of her time was spent with the "hard to reach" kids (i.e., kids that other people couldn't reach). The bird was back in the sky.

The lesson in this story is one I have been taught over and over again. This lady did not need encouragement nearly as much as she needed the opportunity to encourage. Like all of us, an essential part of her mission in life is to encourage people.

Encouragement is a powerful force. This power scares some people. Your desire to encourage *can* get a little out of control. But *there has never been any need for it to stay in control.* If you look deeply enough into your need to encourage, you will find that it is really an expression of love. The only way to contain love is to deny it. If you let yourself feel it, it is uncontainable. This is as it should be.

You may have to wait for someone to encourage you. But you never have to wait to find someone to encourage. You show me a person and I'll show you a person who could benefit from encouragement. The need is always there.

Good encouragement is always sincere. If the sincerity is lacking, it is not encouragement at all but merely manipulation. It can help to have had a good role model. Seeing and feeling genuine encouragement can be quite a learning experience. You learn both the skill and the power. People who spend time with a good encourager develop the talent and desire to pass it on. Encouragement spreads. One might argue that the best way to improve the world is to learn to encourage.

I should make it clear here that encouragement is not the same as praise. Praise is a sign of appreciation that comes after the fact. It's the applause or the congratulations. It's the acknowledgment that you have done a good job. Praise comes *after* an achievement.

Encouragement, on the other hand, comes while someone is approaching their mountain. It's the gentle, and sometimes not so gentle, push that moves one to begin climbing. Encouragement comes *before* the fact. It keeps people moving on their path and in their mission. It's giving courage to someone when his starts running low. It's concerning yourself with the growth of another. It's telling someone that she is a good writer and that she should continue writing her poetry. Or showing your confidence in a friend when he starts to doubt whether he will apply for a promotion.

No one becomes what he or she is meant to be alone. We need other people. We have to travel some of our path alone, but we cannot travel all of it that way. On everyone's road there are mountains that are too high to climb alone. On everyone's journey there is an element of doubt and insecurity. The difference between those who survive and those who do not is often the presence of someone who encourages.

One of the more optimistic theories of human development states that if a child receives a sufficient amount of encouragement, she will internalize an encouraging voice. The voice will then stay with her throughout life. This is not to say that she will no longer need encouragement. What it means is that if she is encouraged often enough and well enough, she will have a voice inside that can support her when no others can be heard. In other words, the encouragement you give someone could last a lifetime.

Encouraging voices, be they internal or external, help move us when we are afraid to move. They also help keep us standing when other voices try to defeat us. Elizabeth David made the point that, "There are people who take the heart right out of you, and there are people who put it back." The people who put it back... these are the folks we need to find. This is the kind of person that each of us needs to become.

Those who hear encouraging voices are those most likely to stay true to themselves. These voices can carry us through the fear and doubt that are inevitable parts of our path. In order to increase the amount of encouragement you hear, you must be willing to do two things. First, you must look for those who will encourage you. These are the people who accept you and appreciate you for who you are and who you can be. They aren't threatened by your gifts or disappointed because you didn't travel in another direction. Encouraging souls aren't prone to envy. Nor do they have a need to control others. They accept you for the person you are meant to be.

Second, you will increase the encouragement in your world as you learn to teach it. Unfortunately, many people have not seen enough of it to know its value or how to implement it. If you boldly step forward as an encourager, you become a role model. Most people learn quickly. It's such a natural process that one acquires it in a very natural way. It's as if we came into the world prepared to encourage.

TEACHERS

Those who encourage provide the heart. Teachers provide the knowledge. Our teachers share with us knowledge on how to get from here to there. They hand down the lessons learned from a thousand mistakes. Certain lessons may need to come through experience. But everything else can come through good teachers.

The term teacher, of course, applies to more than school teachers (although certain school teachers are clearly included in this group). A teacher is anyone who effectively communicates knowledge. There are a lot of good teachers in the world though many are overlooked. Some people spend their lives looking for the wise man on the mountaintop and they fail to see the wise man who lives on the next block. When you look for teachers, you must keep in mind that things are not always as they seem.

One of the best teachers I've ever known was my grandfather. He taught me about life as well as anyone I've ever known. More than anything, he taught me how to learn from life. He showed me that there are valuable lessons everywhere.

As a young man, Grandpop was a boxer. He boxed a lot. Some said he boxed too much. He was, I guess, a little punchy. A genuine character, he definitely had his own idiosyncrasies. He sang songs no one could understand, and he prayed out loud in Gaelic. He spent forever writing a book that had something to do with real estate. The book was never finished, never published. Sadly, I think the manuscript was thrown away when he died.

I thought he was a genius, but I heard the whispers that said he was crazy. After he died, when they read his will, they found something else that made people question the soundness of his mind. He was not wealthy, but he had acquired some land through the years. In his will, he left just about all the land to people who never existed — names he made up, I suppose. There was, however, one exception. He left a piece of land near Atlantic City to me.

As is often the case, people thought Grandpop was crazy because they couldn't understand what he was saying. He also scared a few people who did understand him because he talked about life — a subject that frightens some of us.

Grandpop talked about life, and he usually did so through sports metaphors. He had been a boxer and a long distance runner in his day and he liked to use these two events to explain the human condition. He also spoke quite frequently in the language of baseball.

The world according to Grandpop began with the jab. He taught that you should always keep jabbing. Jab! Jab! Jab! The big punch will come in its own time. It's the repeated small jabs you throw that set up the knockout. LESSON: It's the relentless attention to the small things that lead to success. Never stop seizing opportunities, no matter how small they may seem at the time.

Both his running and his boxing served as grist for stories about never giving up. A lot of these were short stories. "If you get knocked down, you get right back up," he'd say, while crouched in a boxer's stance with a mouthful of chewing tobacco. Or he would lift his head, change sports, and say, "You just keep running!" LESSON: There's no reason to even think about giving up.

He spent every summer night in a dark room listening to the Phillies games on a radio that carried more static than play-by-play. My parents bought him a color television to make life a little easier. For his own reasons, Grandpop preferred the static and the darkness.

He also liked to yell at the radio. More specifically, he would voice his objections to certain coaching decisions. There was, I remember, one fascinating point I heard him make repeatedly. He'd often get upset when managers would come out of the dugout to talk to their pitchers when the pitchers got into trouble. Grandpop had a lot of faith in people it seems. Many times I'd hear him scream at the radio, insisting that a coach go back into the dugout. "Let him throw, he'll work it out!" LESSON: Sometimes an effort to help can be premature and harmful. Give people an opportunity to work problems out by themselves. It builds confidence. (This lesson has been especially helpful to me as a therapist.)

I could go on and on about the world according to Grandpop. But the point I'm really trying to make is not about any one of his teachings. It's about teachers. They are not walking around with huge signs that say TEACHER, but they are out there nonetheless. There are teachers capable of giving you a single crucial lesson, and there are others with a great deal of important advice to pass on. There are master teachers who can teach you the process of learning. These educators show you *how* to learn. Once you have learned how to learn, then every experience in your life becomes a teacher.

As you learn and learn and learn, you will find that certain questions are special to you. These emerge as more important than the rest. These questions not only capture your curiosity, they also capture your spirit. They grow on you and into you. They pull you along. Now you are looking for special teachers. You probably will find that no one teacher has all the pieces to your puzzle. More likely, you will have several, perhaps many, to give you what you need.

In order to travel successfully on the road to you, it is necessary that you develop an eye for good teachers. It's wonderful to search for knowledge. But in so doing we can miss the people who supply the knowledge. In looking for knowledge, we are also looking for people. Much, perhaps most, of what we learn in life will come by way of others.

Experiences with the shadow and dragon are examples of knowledge gained from direct experience. The yearning that is produced by a calling is also a firsthand experience. There is no question that the lessons life teaches us firsthand are vital to our development. The knowledge we gain from our fellow travelers, however, takes us much farther than we could otherwise go. Without the wisdom of other human beings, we can be no wiser than our years. We couldn't possibly be. When we learn from other people, we open ourselves to the wisdom of the ages. We open ourselves to all the lessons learned by other travelers on other paths. We open ourselves to those who can observe our path from the outside — a perspective that can be very enlightening.

Good teachers are like good leaders, they will not take you too far. They won't impose their missions upon you. They understand that you have your own journey with your own tasks to complete. Good teachers are sensitive to the questions that you feel are most important. They teach what they can and are, themselves, always looking to learn. The best teachers, by the way, teach only what they can. They maintain the honesty to say, "I don't know."

Teachers bring you knowledge. When you receive knowledge you are empowered. As we have established in the earlier chapters, empowerment is one half of our most powerful growing experiences. The other half is humility. A teacher brings you empowerment (knowledge), and if we look closer, we find that this same soul can also carry humility to you. The humility a good teacher brings you comes in the form of gratitude. When you feel grateful to someone for teaching you, you have been humbled.

Gratitude is a form of humility. It is the realization and acceptance that what you are becoming is, at least partially, someone else's achievement. Furthermore, this is a debt that can never be fully repaid (nor does it have to be). Instead, it is an understanding that becomes permanent. One could argue persuasively that gratitude is the most important gift a teacher gives you.

The most fortunate soul is the one who has many to thank. This person has been given a great deal. This individual is also blessed because gratitude keeps people connected. Gratitude creates a bond that is woven out of love, humility, and respect. Such a bond is really a lifeline. It empowers and humbles. It builds us and grounds us.

At this point in one's journey, the priority is to find good teachers. As time passes, that priority will change. Eventually one's goal will be to *be* a good teacher. The lessons learned at this stage must be handed down. At that point in life, one will be looking for good students.

CONCLUSION

People need people. In the process of finding who you are meant to be, you benefit from those willing to encourage you. You, like everyone else, will face moments of doubt and uncertainty. These are fertile grounds for fear. Feeling that push of a strong voice can make the difference between advance and retreat. Receiving encouragement can fill your sail with wind.

Giving encouragement fills a spiritual need. If you are willing to give your courage to others, you will never be in short supply. Courage was never meant to be hoarded. It is to be used and given away. When it is, it is always there.

Part of your path you must travel alone. But you do not need to travel all of it alone. Your relationships can bring you courage, knowledge, love, and gratitude. They can empower and humble you.

The need to bond with fellow travelers is so basic and natural that it defies explanation. Fortunately, we need no explanation. We simply need to accept the fact that on a physical, psychological, and spiritual level, we need to connect with other human beings. It is through these bonds that we become more than we ever could alone.

If you hope to travel successfully on the road to you, you will need to look for those who have messages for you. These people are your guides, your teachers. Some will bring you small bits of information. Others are capable of delivering to you a great deal of knowledge. Remember, you will have learned little from these souls until you feel gratitude toward them.

As you learn, pay close attention to the questions that are emerging within you. These are your questions. No matter how wise your teachers have been, none of them will be able to answer these special questions. These are *your* questions. These are the questions *you* are to answer. Learn everything you can. Find the best teachers. But know that you must take responsibility for your answers.

The road to you will go through other people. If you isolate yourself, you will not get there. Some people have an easier time fighting their dragons and exploring their shadow than they do connecting with their fellow travelers. Still, this connection must be made. For here lies the courage and knowledge you need, the courage and knowledge you lack.

Ultimately, the lesson you learn from your fellow travelers is how much people need people. As you get stronger, you become more aware of your neediness. As this lesson takes root in your soul, you become more than a student. You become a student and a teacher. And as this process unfolds, your spirit grows deeper and deeper.

CHAPTER SIX

INSIGHT & INNOCENCE

There is a Native American tale that explains how the earth was prepared for human beings. This legend speaks to the nature of insight and wisdom and where they are sometimes found.

According to this story, shortly before humans were to be placed on earth, the Great Spirit sent three spirits to earth to prepare for the arrival of humans. As soon as they arrived, the spirits got right to work. All went smoothly until they encountered the question: "Where will we put the essential truths of life?" They discussed this and all agreed that these truths should be earned. They wanted only those with true character and perseverance to reach this knowledge.

One of the spirits suggested that the essential truths be placed at the bottom of the deepest sea. Then only the most daring and dedicated human beings would be able to reach them. The other two spirits listened to this and then reflected upon it.

The second spirit then recommended that the fundamental truths be placed on top of the highest mountain. If they are there, the spirit reasoned, only the bravest and most clever explorers could attain them. Again, the other spirits listened and reflected.

Finally, the third — known to be the wisest — spirit spoke. He said, "Maybe we should put these truths deep inside each human being. Only a person of true character will dare look there." The other two spirits agreed immediately. Thus, according to legend, it was decided that when we human beings arrived on earth, we would come with valuable knowledge planted deep within us. Whether or not we tap this knowledge, however, is up to each of us. One can live a lifetime without ever coming into contact with it.

Insight is the process of putting together what we know on all our different levels. It means integrating the various pieces of ourselves. Developing insight means developing one's capacity for understanding. It begins as you start understanding things you could never put into words (even if you still can't put them into words). Insight comes as you understand what you already know.

When someone develops insight, he no longer has to depend on other people in order to learn. This does not at all diminish his desire to learn from others. In fact, insight usually increases one's appreciation of good teachers. When someone develops insight, she builds a love for learning. This person is eager to consider the lessons other people have to share. She is, however, no longer dependent on them. Developing insight increases one's freedom.

One of the myths about insight is that it is always a wonderful experience. It's one of life's more significant paradoxes — insight sometimes leads to confusion. One of the things you can become aware of is how much you don't know. Insight can lead to confusion which can, in turn, lead to deeper insight. In other words, if you face your ignorance honestly, your ignorance becomes a form of insight.

Insight doesn't always lead directly to answers. It may first take you to those important questions we discussed in the last chapter. Your special questions point you in a particular direction. This is a voyage of insight. You feel the questions before you find the answers.

One of the other myths about ignorance is that it is always an awful experience. In truth, feeling an important question without having its answer can be exhilarating. It can be challenging, awakening, and it can be the bugle call to grow. Ignorance can be the screaming yet loving voice within you that shouts, "This is what I need to know!"

When you become secure enough to welcome your encounters with ignorance, no matter how bright you are or how good your teachers are, and in spite of all the wisdom you may have brought into the world with you, you will encounter ignorance in yourself. You can run from it with denial or arrogance, or you can face it with the gratitude you would afford a master teacher.

During my first few years after graduate school, I began making professional and public presentations. Soon after, I started teaching graduate students. During these years, I worked with one fundamental rule: *Know Everything!* For each presentation I prepared and prepared and prepared, believing the sky would fall if someone in the audience asked me something that I couldn't answer. I got pretty good at this. My fear of appearing inadequate made me quite knowledgeable. Funny thing though, as I felt more and more secure, I became more and more bored. I knew all the old facts. In fact, I was stuck in the facts. I couldn't see the new questions.

Fortunately, my perspective gradually changed. For many, myself included, boredom is more aversive than fear. As time passed, I began to love what I had feared the most. I came to love the questions that I couldn't answer. Each one killed boredom. Each opened a new door, a door to new knowledge. I was no longer afraid of ignorance. I could now look a student in the eye and say, "I have no idea. But what a beautiful question!" First, the boredom left. Then the fear disappeared. And both were replaced with gratitude. I became grateful to everyone who asked me a question I couldn't answer.

A Zen aphorism says, "When the mind is ready, a teacher appears." The mind becomes ready when it accepts ignorance and, just as importantly, accepts it as a starting point. The sage and the fool are both ignorant. But they live their ignorance differently. The fool fights the awareness of ignorance. When he is forced to see it, he treats it as his destination, something to wallow in. The sage welcomes his ignorance as the door to new learning. To the sage, ignorance is an invitation to knowledge and gratitude.

This state is not particularly hard to find. You can see it in just about every small child. We call it innocence. Small children are gracefully ignorant. They have no need to know, only a need to find out. There's no shame in not knowing, but there is tremendous satisfaction in learning. As long as the innocence stays alive, the thirst for knowledge will thrive. When the innocence dies and people become ashamed of not knowing, they no longer dance gracefully with their ignorance. Instead, they come to fear and hate it.

People who lose their innocence do not need to create it. They need to retrieve it. They need to go back and re-acquaint themselves with the person they once were. When they do, they had better be prepared to answer a lot of questions. The child has much to ask them and much to teach them. The child's questions serve both these ends.

One's mind is ready when it is motivated by what it does not know. The mind is ready when this state creates a hunger, a hunger that can be felt throughout one's being. The hunger is completely unknown to some who are so far from it that they feel no motivation.

The hunger can begin at any time. As it builds, it leads you to the teachers and experiences that are valuable to your journey. Your curiosity plays a large part in leading you to you. When you are lost in life, it can be helpful to *follow your questions.* Your questions are as unique as you are. When you touch upon your special questions, you will feel a drive for answers. This drive for answers is a part of your mission. You don't have to explain or defend it. Your questions are a part of who you are and they will help lead you to who you are meant to be.

Insight is not only about finding answers. It is also about finding ignorance and motivation. It's also about finding your special questions. These can come to you at any time. Sometimes they come while you are looking for them and sometimes they come while you are looking for something else. But if there is one kind of experience that is most likely to bring insight, it may be the experience of stillness.

Stillness

Stillness has a way of setting the stage for insight. If the stage is properly set, insight seems called to it. Insight seldom forces its way into your consciousness. Instead, it's something that you have to prepare for and then work with once it reaches you.

Stillness is both a place and a state of being. It's the place you find yourself in when all the noises and distractions have gone away. It's the place where silence can carry messages. Some find this happening naturally, early in life. Others stumble across it later on, perhaps by accident. And then there are people who are led to stillness by their teachers.

Stillness is a good place to hear what your spirit is saying. The spirit can probably speak as loud as it wants, but when you create stillness you are asking it to express itself. It's not only the quiet that attracts the spiritual side, it is also the act of asking your spirit to emerge that makes it feel welcome.

It sounds simple. And for many people it is. For many, though, it is anything but. There are countless individuals who will not tolerate tranquility, people who feel a desperate need for noise and distraction. They call any hint of stillness "unbearable boredom" and fight their way out of it in much the same way a trapped animal fights its cage.

People fight and flee tranquility for several reasons. Basically, they fear what they might hear. This is especially true of those who have not adequately worked through their shadow. They know that within them they have material that upsets them. Instead of bringing it into the light of conscious awareness, they contain it in their psychic dungeon. Tranquility threatens this arrangement. It lifts the energy needed to keep the dungeon closed. Stillness gives the shadow the opportunity to empty itself.

This emptying is rarely a surprise. We know what it takes to repress the unacceptable parts of ourselves. We also know — at some level — how this material can escape. As long as we choose to repress our dark side, then we will have to avoid those activities that might empty the shadow. Finding stillness is one such activity.

Yes, stillness threatens repression. It can put you in touch with all your unfinished business — the loss you've never quite gotten over, the talent you've never developed, the applause you've never received. Stillness may show you the next step in your calling, a step that could be risky or pull you into a brand new world. Furthermore, stillness could put you in touch with the need to change aspects of your life that give you the most security.

If you are not ready to deal with what stillness may bring you, then you may not be ready for insight. Your flaws will not block insight. It's the unwillingness to accept flaws that will keep you afraid of what lives inside you. If your fear keeps you from looking within, you miss all the wisdom there.

Those who welcome an awareness of what lies within are more comfortable with stillness. They find it in their own ways. Maybe it's an early morning walk or watching the sun set. Maybe it's painting or simply sitting in a quiet room. Or it could be relaxing by a campfire or kneeling quietly in church.

Finding stillness, like finding insight itself, is both an active and a passive process. It requires an eagerness to know and a willingness to wait. Sometimes the first lesson that comes out of stillness is how to wait. Someone willing to wait is someone willing to live with the ways of the universe. There are many wonderful phenomena whose arrival we cannot control. The best we can do is prepare ourselves for their arrival. Waiting quietly can be the best form of preparation.

With physical sleep, noise usually serves to wake us up. Whether it is something deliberate like the alarm clock or something unplanned like the neighbors, loud sounds tend to bring us back to the land of the living. With our psycho-spiritual side, the opposite is more often true. In this realm, we can be awakened by silence. In the quiet, the mind and the spirit meet and integrate. This is the beginning of wisdom.

Wisdom cannot be handed to you. You cannot buy it. It comes as you integrate the knowledge within you with the knowledge given to you by your teachers and your experiences. I call the beginning stage of wisdom "insight." It is here where knowledge begins to come together in a greater whole. At this point you still have much to learn and yet you know more than you know. Ultimately, as insight continues to grow into deeper wisdom, it blossoms into an awakening that is often called enlightenment.

Insight — the beginning of wisdom — is formed in stillness. Silence arouses the psyche and the spirit. In *Wherever You Go There You Are*, Jon Kabat-Zinn describes this process with simple elegance. He explains how meditation — one means of achieving insight — can lead to insight:

> It is about coming to realize that you are on a path whether you like it or not, namely, the path that is your life. Meditation may help us see that this path we call life has direc-

tion; that it is always unfolding, moment by moment; and that what happens now, in this moment, influences what happens next.[1]

All effective methods of achieving stillness, including meditation, help you rid yourself of noise. Some of the loudest noise can come from within. Take, for example, your rigid biases. These are the beliefs that throw tantrums if they are put aside for even the shortest time. These beliefs can take so much of your energy that it's as if they have taken on a life of their own. If they see that you might look at the world with energetic curiosity, these beliefs begin to filibuster. Their objective is to upset the stillness that leads to insight. With insight there is often change. A willingness to change and grow makes stillness feel beautiful.

When you achieve stillness, you begin to see things as they are. As you see things as they are, you become capable of seeing yourself as you are. When you see yourself as you are, you begin to see yourself as you could be. And when you see who you are, you begin to see who you are meant to be.

LEARNING THE LANGUAGE OF LIFE

Early in my career as a therapist, a mentor gave me a piece of advice that immediately improved the way I treated my clients. This simple lesson has been more valuable to me than I could ever express. The gem he handed me was this: "All human beings have their own language. If you want to help someone, you have to begin by learning their language."

When I first heard this it confused me and yet, at the same time, it made sense. It was something I knew, but never realized. As I became aware that everyone uses language in their own way, I began to listen better. I not only listened to the words, but how they used the words. I listened for their favorite words and phrases. Almost at once I found that if I could understand an individual's language, I could reach a much deeper understanding of his or her world.

Gradually I extended this lesson. I came to the insight that in order to understand anything, I first have to learn its language. This meant abandoning the egocentric notion that everything and everyone in the universe speaks *my* language. I had to comprehend that understanding life means understanding languages besides my own.

Nature seems to have its own language. One might even argue that everything within nature has its own tongue. If you take this thinking far enough, you come to the question: "Does God have His own language?" I don't think anyone really knows. There are so many implications to this. But if I had to offer an opinion, I might suggest that every language is a part of God's language. He speaks them all. I might add that with every language we learn, we become more proficient in speaking with God.

As we learn the languages of the universe, we grow closer to all that makes up our world. Everything that we connect with teaches us something. We learn from what we connect with, and we learn something from within ourselves. For example, if while sitting on the shore you feel yourself falling into a relationship with the ocean, you will find that the ocean teaches you something. I can't tell you what that may be; nature has so many things to pass on. And if you feel yourself connecting with that ocean, you will also learn something from within yourself. This insight may relate to what you have learned from the ocean. Thus there are two lessons: one from the outside, one from within.

Insights are often the lessons you learn from within that help you accommodate what life is trying to teach you. Insight prepares you to learn. Insight is frequently a product of stillness, and yet insight also creates its own stillness. It creates teachable moments when you are reminded that you don't know everything. With this humbling awareness, though, comes the empowering conviction that you are capable of learning life's most important lessons.

Once you begin to appreciate that life is filled with languages, you soon realize that similarities exist among these languages. Once you realize the diversity, you become more impressed by the common themes. One such theme deserves special mention here. People describe life in a variety of ways. And yet through the ages and across cultures, one particular description appears over and over again. It seems that all languages have described life as a journey. Life is a dynamic process where one travels toward something. If there were no destination, then life would be only movement, aimless and confusing. A journey, however, implies a destination, a place or a state that we move toward.

The awareness of a destination is one of the most important insights we have in life. It begins when we feel the yearning. This starts us moving and looking down the road. After the movement begins, we build our characters by facing obstacles that challenge our body, mind, and spirit. Once we pass through these tests of character, we realize that we are more prepared to learn than we have ever been. With this in mind, we look for teachers who can provide us with answers and offer us encouragement to continue to seek knowledge.

Insight follows a genuine, honest desire to learn. When someone has reached this stage in the journey of life, he starts to understand that there is indeed a destination on the road he is traveling. We all travel a path in life. But this doesn't mean we need to — or should — spend our lives as travelers. There comes a time when one arrives. Once you reach your destination, your heart continues to beat, your mind continues to thrive, and your spirit soars more than ever. When you reach your destination on your journey of life you grow roots, you drop anchor. When you reach this destination, you will have become the person you are meant to be. You then go about living your life this way.

Perhaps the most important insight that comes during this stage of the road to you is that the road does not go on forever. There is a destination. The flower, if it is nurtured properly, will eventually blossom. When this insight occurs, the journey changes. It becomes more real with a clearer purpose. You are not just traveling for the sake of traveling. You are instead traveling to a place that is meant for you. A place that is waiting for you and hoping you get there.

When you realize there is a person you are meant to be, that you have what it takes to fulfill your calling, you receive an additional flow of energy. It's like when you travel to the mountains. Your trip may have drained you completely, but as soon as you see the mountains, the energy gets turned on. Even though they may still be a long way off, seeing them reassures you that your journey has a destination. Destinations provide energy! An exhausted crew finds strength as soon as it sees shore.

As you learn the languages of life, you come to understand the signs along the road. You start to learn about the place up ahead. It takes form as you learn about it. This is the place where you will do your best work, your life's work. Learning the languages of life helps you reach your destination and, just as importantly, it will assist you once you reach your destination. Knowing how to converse with the universe will make you more effective in your work.

With every language you learn, you connect with more potential teachers. As you become more proficient with languages, your teachers will be virtually everywhere. For example, once you understand that nature has its own languages, nature opens up to you as an endless stream of master teachers.

Every master teacher you meet releases new questions in

you. As the number of your teachers grows, so will the number of your questions. In this stage where you learn of ignorance and insight, you take stock of what you know and what you don't know. Furthermore, you place a value on both. You place a value on certain knowledge as well as particular unanswered questions. Here you are looking for those special questions that remain unsolved. These special questions compose much of what is left on the road to you. An acceptance of ignorance is a prerequisite to finding the questions you need. Accepting yourself as lost is often the first step in finding your way home.

When people reach this point, they are ready to look at the big questions of life. These kinds of questions are many. What is the force that is calling me? Why have I been wounded? What is a good life? What is a good person? How can I contribute most to humanity? How will I be remembered after I die? Am I where I really belong? These are just a few examples of the types of questions that may emerge or reemerge during this time.

During this stage, a person pursues life's bigger questions. If one stays with these questions and faces them honestly and courageously, one becomes a simple scholar. A simple scholar is a person who, while aware of his ignorance, searches for the wisdom needed to become the person he is meant to be. He may not know how many bones there are in the body or the capitals of all the South American countries. He may not have spent a lot of time in school. But he has learned enough of the languages of life to lead him to the questions that matter most. The simple scholar looks for knowledge about how he is to live his life.

Once you learn the languages of life, a fundamental lesson presents itself repeatedly to you. Life does not last forever. What you are to accomplish must be done in a limited amount of time. The awareness of death keeps you from spending your days stuck on questions that have no bearing on your mission. Insight is not about mindlessly creating questions. It's about finding the questions that matter most to you and searching for their answers. No one lives long enough to answer every question. But life gives us time to answer some. Also, the awareness that life does not last forever prompts us to become active in our pursuit of knowledge.

Viktor Frankl explained this well. Frankl believed that as human beings, our most important psychological need is to find meaning in our lives. He insisted that everyone has a purpose in life. This meaning does not have to be *created*; it has already been created and therefore must simply be *found*. The meaning of our lives is not something we make up; it's quite real and we must find it. Frankl, however, made the observation that many people never find their meaning because they are not willing to do more than sit back and ask, "What is the meaning of my life?" Frankl insisted that it is not enough to ask the question. *Life asks us the question; it's our job to find the answer.*

When you identify the questions that matter most to you, your inner compass begins to point. When you accept the implications of your mortality, your inner compass begins to point with urgency. St. Augustine once said, "It is only in the face of death that man's self is born." The simple scholar knows that her time is limited. This is perhaps the most basic lesson in life and yet so many of us manage to miss it.

We need not dwell on death. We need only be aware of it. The anxiety created by this awareness helps fuel our journey to the person we are meant to be. It pushes us to be active in our pursuit of love and knowledge. The awareness of a limited life-span urges us to focus on the questions and issues that matter most. There is a reason that certain questions are important to you. They matter to you because they are part of your calling. Your most powerful questions are part of your calling.

EXPERIENCE

There is more to life than you will ever be told. You will need to know more than what other people can teach you. As important as teachers are, they cannot give you all that you need to know.

Many of the most valuable lessons in life can only be acquired through experience. In other words, some things you have to learn for yourself, by yourself. Experience is a hard teacher. Some say it is the toughest teacher of all because it gives you the test before it teaches you the lesson. Often, experience is what you acquire when you learn "the hard way." In truth, sometimes the hard way is the only way.

In order to learn from experience, you must decide to make learning a way of life. Everyone has learning experiences, but not everyone learns from them. Some folks learn the lesson long after the experience. Others never find the gold. Those who become accustomed to learning from what they live are enriched by everything they encounter.

Knowledge consists of what you have learned from *what you have been taught and what you have not been taught*. Experience teaches you all the important lessons that no one can teach you. For instance, no one can teach you about feelings. To really learn about feelings, you have to go there yourself. People can encourage you to go there but they can never tell you what will happen when you do. And once you jump into the land of feelings, you find yourself learning through all your senses. (This is typical with experiential learning.) The more senses that are involved, the more likely it is that you will retain what you've acquired. This is one of the reasons experiential learning can be so powerful. It surrounds us. If we let it, it can fill us.

This is the case with feelings. They have the ability to fill us like few other forces can. Their lessons are many, perhaps as many as there are people. They affect the physical, psychological, and spiritual dimensions of our beings. They can push hard to share their wisdom. You need to feel before you can live. You need to feel before you can pray.

Good teachers know there is knowledge they cannot teach. They encourage their students to explore the world. A classroom can be a wonderful place or it can be a refuge for cowards. You have to be able to learn without teachers. Your path in life is unique. You will encounter experiences along the way that no one else ever has. No one can warn you about them because no one has ever experienced them.

Goethe once remarked that we see what we know. We prepare ourselves to see what we expect to see. This preparation can be so powerful that we may see only those things we expect to see. Once this mindset sets in, the world runs out of newness. Everything gets explained in old theories and formulas. The world loses its freshness. Experience then teaches us little. It merely confirms what we already know.

This sad state of affairs can be explained in different ways. More than anything, though, this situation is caused by the loss of innocence. When we lose our innocence, the world grows old. The awe and wonder leave. Miracles fade away. Curiosity may not die but it loses its push.

Innocence is a state of being where you are comfortable with your ignorance. There is no shame in asking the simplest questions. Bitterness and cynicism can't stick to the soul that has maintained its innocence. Take a walk in nature with a three-year-old and see the wide eyed fascination of innocence. Small children see what the scientists miss. At this age most children are still true to their nature. We come into the world eager to learn from experience. This eagerness can persist for a lifetime. Or it can be misunderstood to be only a quality of childhood and eventually put in our basements when adulthood arrives.

Many of us abandon our innocence because it threatens

something very precious to the adult world — control. We like control. We want to be able to predict and control everything that is awaiting us around the bend. To an extent this is healthy. We all want to feel safe. But when our need for control reaches the point that it cuts us off from new experiences — either by avoiding them or denying the ones we can't avoid — our journey ends. The road continues. Our destination still waits down that road. But no one gets there until they notice the newness. Until they learn from experience.

The wisest people I have ever known have all kept their innocence. Some had to retrieve it after losing it. Then upon retrieving their innocence, they graduated from know-it-alls to simple scholars. At the heart of being a simple scholar is a love for the fact that there is always more to learn.

Everyone's path is filled with experiences, each with its own knowledge to share. But among the lessons, there is one that shapes character perhaps more than any other. This is the lesson we call morality. Morality is often taught by teachers but it really only becomes a part of us through experience. Morality is not a part of us until we act on it. We don't recognize the rights of others until we feel a connection to them. We don't practice self-respect until we feel respect for ourselves. If we act morally because we are told to do so, then our morality is conformity — something that will likely be violated when one's authorities are not looking or when authorities with new values come along. Real morality is something we learn from life; it is something we follow because we decide it is the right way to live.

Those who have enough innocence to feel the real power of their life experiences will have an advantage here as well. Morality has power. But it may only impact those willing to be moved by human decency, people who feel awe when they see goodness. These are the people who have kept their innocence alive.

Those who lose their innocence may also lose their morality.

CONCLUSION

As we open ourselves to learning, we feel pulled more than ever to a destination. If we are learning, we will feel the yearning. During this stage of insight we realize that our time is limited. We have to identify the questions that matter most and move toward answering them. These questions are a part of who we are. Answering them is a part of who we are meant to be. These special questions that come from within us are the same questions that life is asking us.

At many points in our lives we will be led by our questions. There are, of course, other forces that move us, forces such as love, belonging, self-esteem, and survival. But everyone has these needs. Your special questions are unique. Everyone has their questions but you may be the only one given your special collection of mysteries to solve.

Questions survive only in people who can live peacefully with ignorance. A person who denies his ignorance will never find his mission or who he is meant to be. Finding what we need to know begins with accepting that we don't know. A peaceful acceptance of ignorance is not the same as complacency. A peaceful acceptance of ignorance is a starting point. This is the innocence that prepares the way for learning. It's one of those important paradoxes of life: once we think we know everything, we're lost. Our questions help keep us on course.

Those who maintain their innocence — or retrieve it after it has been lost — dance gracefully with their ignorance. They revel in the very thing that fools dread. Their innocence gives them the power to see what others cannot and the courage to feel and ask what others will not. They live in a friendly world that guides them as a loving teacher would.

As we learn to love our innocence, we become more insightful. Innocence frees us to ask our questions, no matter how simple they may sound. Innocence is there to guide us; it has no ambition to impress.

The road to you has a destination. It does not go on endlessly. It is at this stage of your journey, however, that you begin to understand that, should you reach that destination, you will not be all-powerful or all-knowing. You will indeed be empowered along the way. But you will also be humbled. And when you become the person you are meant to be, you will find that you are both weak and strong. You will find that you have become an enlightened innocent.

CHAPTER SEVEN

DOUBT & ENLIGHTENMENT

Most of us lose our innocence at one time or another. Often this loss is part of the wound we receive from our dragons or the price we pay for looking into our shadows. Many of us abandon our innocence and consider this the cost of surviving in our jungle. At the time, though, we don't realize how much we are losing when we say good-bye to our innocence.

Fortunately, innocence lost does not necessarily mean innocence gone forever. Denying your innocence is like denying your spirit; the denial will not kill it. And like your spirit, when you return to your innocence, your life changes significantly.

Retrieving your innocence is like shedding an old skin. A new self emerges. It's not a new self with all the answers; rather it's a new self that loves to look for answers. The new self does not accept other people's stories as the final word. When people retrieve their innocence, they are less interested in hearing other people's stories about God and more interested in meeting Him themselves. Curiosity means your intellect wants to know something. Innocence means your entire being wants to know.

But those who retrieve their innocence soon run into a challenge. They encounter the thing that may have caused them to part with their innocence in the first place — doubt.

DOUBT

Innocence refuses to accept the notion that you know all there is to know. There is always more. Consequently, innocence brings with it doubt. It's not an annoying or frustrating doubt; it's a doubt that reminds us that there might be more. It's not a doubt that disqualifies all that we have learned; it's a doubt that reminds us that what we have already learned can lead us farther. Doubt can be motivating. Still, doubt interferes with our sense of control. We would prefer to be sure. Toward that end, we are tempted to create shallow philosophies and explanations that convince us that nothing could shake our certainty. Ironically, though, this certainty that we sometimes worship is a punishing ruler. It makes us bored and bitter. It takes our vitality and gives us only illusion. In the final analysis, this is all we really control — our illusions.

Boredom and bitterness indicate that one is far from where one needs to be. If these symptoms are not tended to, they spread. As this condition deteriorates, it produces a more painful, debilitating form of doubt. This is different than the doubt that is inherent in innocence. Innocence helps prepare you for doubt; it may even help you enjoy doubt. The doubt that comes from boredom and bitterness is anything but invited. This is the reality that crashes through the illusion of control. It is the voice that says, "You are in the wrong place."

The part of us that wants complete control fights the doubt. Our innocence invites it into our lives. As a result, we can know two very different types of doubt — productive and nonproductive. We experience nonproductive doubt when we refuse to allow productive doubt into our lives. If we only fight our doubts, they become unhealthy. Like any other experience, if we can only fight it, we will never learn from it. Doubt remains until we learn its message. We can be so intent upon denying it that we are more willing to call it depression or anxiety, more medical and less personal conditions. We can have a hard time admitting that sometimes we get a little lost.

We make doubt productive when we accept it as a teaching experience. Doubt is part of our inner compass. Doubt indicates that we need to focus our attention on certain aspects of our lives, aspects that may be extremely important to us. During the course of most good marriages, spouses have their doubts about their union. People with the strongest faith are often those most accepting of their periods of doubt.

Doubt may lead you to change or it may lead you to a much stronger commitment to the road you're already on. If you are strong enough to maintain your innocence, then you will be healthy enough to welcome doubt into your life. Doubt is not a destructive force unless you make it one. If you invite it into your life, it will be a venerable guide.

When you accept doubt into your life, you make several important character adjustments. First, arrogance melts away. Doubt is a great equalizer. It takes the "all" out of know-it-all. Then, as your ego becomes smaller, life becomes larger. The newness returns, and with it, it brings awe, majesty, and wonder. No longer is a sunrise just another sunrise. No two infants are the same. Music becomes more powerful. When you bring innocence back into your life, you accept a certain amount of doubt. Also included in the package is an enhanced awareness and appreciation of beauty.

When the size of your ego and your need for control shrink to the point where they no longer control your life, you feel a genuine sense of freedom. You are now free to become what you are meant to be. You allow yourself to accept life on its terms instead of refusing to deal with it unless it speaks your language and conforms to your demands.

Innocence is a graceful dance with doubt. Sometimes you lead. Sometimes you follow. If you learn from your doubt, then you will probably move on. You will grow farther and stronger. If, however, you refuse to accept your doubt as a learning experience, you will be condemned to repeat it. The road to you passes through stages of doubt, sometimes through the deep all-consuming doubt that can be every bit as ominous as any dragon you may have faced. And like the dragon, you cannot continue on your path until you have learned the lesson of your doubt.

These are the lessons that join doubt and enlightenment. Those willing to face their doubts enter a time of reflection. The intensity of this reflection often matches the intensity of the doubt. The reflection brought on by doubt can lead to breakthroughs in a person's psychological and spiritual functioning. Doubt may be the darkness but reflection leads to the Light. Not only are we enhanced each time we see the Light; we are empowered by learning how to reach the Light.

When you dance elegantly with ignorance and doubt, you fall naturally into the art of reflection. As you become more and more comfortable with reflection, important changes occur. It is here that you really begin to take ownership of the choices you are making. You now understand that, even without the total control you once may have convinced yourself was yours, you still are the one who is making your choices. You know down to your soul that you are responsible for what you do with your life. Paradoxically, as you feel this freedom, you may feel pulled in your direction more intensely than you ever have.

This is the point where people frequently make the *big moves*. The discontented accountant buys the restaurant he has dreamed about. The middle-aged housewife applies to law school. The physician who has felt burned out, perhaps for years, awakens to the awareness that she is, in fact, on the right road. So instead of spending her days daydreaming about what she may call "the good life," she comes to realize that for her the most wonderful path in the universe is the one she has taken for granted. It's funny how your life can change when you feel appreciation and gratitude for that life. It's also interesting how the despair that can grow out of doubt can be, ultimately, freeing. Some suggest that you have to hit bottom before you are ready to make the big changes in your life. While I don't believe that this is true for everyone, it seems that it is a valid observation for many of us. There are indeed many individuals who come away from rock bottom with a determination they've never known before. Maybe it's because they have developed confidence in their ability to survive. Or perhaps there's more to it.

LESSONS FROM ROCK BOTTOM

There are small doubts, the ones that cause moments of reflection. Then there are the larger, more troubling doubts. These don't go away in moments. They hang on, immune to your efforts to chase them away. When they grow beyond a certain point, they turn into despair. Doubt, you see, can lead to enlightenment or it can lead to despair — the place I will here call Rock Bottom. And sometimes, as we shall see, the voyage that begins with doubt and ends in enlightenment, travels through despair.

One of the most troubling characteristics of Rock Bottom is that when you reach it, you are given serious doubts about whether you will ever leave there. It's as if you have arrived at a place where you will spend what remains of your life. Rock Bottom presents itself as a life — or should I say life-ending — sentence. Consequently, the typical first response upon arriving here is the thought of death or self-destruction. No one wants to spend their days here. Those who fight off the immediate urge to destroy themselves resign themselves to a future without hope or happiness. I'll never get better, they conclude. They surrender to a life of hard labor.

Once they arrive in Rock Bottom some people kill themselves and some people build a house. Those who build a house see no way out so they start trying to grow roots into the rock. Some of these people deal with the loneliness inherent in this place by attempting to pull others down with them. For some individuals it's true: misery loves company.

But it doesn't have to be this way. Suicide and surrender are not the ways to deal with Rock Bottom. As devastating as this situation can be, it does not have the power to defeat anyone. Self-destruction is something you have to do to yourself. Similarly, self-repair is also something you will have to do largely by yourself. Rock Bottom is a place you go by yourself. You are alone. Once you begin to leave this place you will have opportunities for support and assistance (should you decide to look for them). But the first few steps you take out of Rock Bottom you have to take all by yourself.

You begin to take these steps when you are ready. We have our own unique needs and some of us need to spend more time here than others do. If one doesn't learn enough from Rock Bottom while one is there, one may fall back later to finish the lesson. Like all experiences in life, this horrible place has its lessons. Some of these lessons will be realized at the time, others not until much later.

Rock Bottom may have as many lessons as there are people who go there. But there are also lessons that tend to repeat themselves. Here are a few of Rock Bottom's most repeated teachings.

1. People live in Rock Bottom day to day. For a while you may not even realize that you are surviving. It may not feel like surviving. But this is often the first lesson. At some point you realize that you have been surviving. It may be too soon for you to be comfortable calling yourself a survivor. So you merely begin with the

awakening that you have been surviving. You may have had thoughts of suicide and you know others have taken this route. But you are still alive.

2. At Rock Bottom you learn that you can feel more deeply and more fully than you ever thought possible. The reality is much more profound than the story.

3. Surprisingly, many people have their callings clarified for them while they are here. Maybe it is because of the stillness of Rock Bottom. Or maybe it's the aloneness. With fewer voices speaking in your ears, you may have an easier time hearing the really important voices. Whatever the reason, when all is lost, you may find what you need most. When you feel most alone, you may perhaps for the first time — feel a Presence.

4. For many people, spirituality begins to thrive when they are at their lowest point. Another paradox. Many people meet their Higher Power when they hit the depths of despair. Here too, there are many reasons for this. But maybe more than anything else, so many people touch God while at Rock Bottom because this is the first time in their lives that they let go of the conviction that they are their own higher power.

5. Although people frequently connect with God while at their lowest point, they also learn that God is not there to miraculously lift them to higher ground. You can walk with God, but to do so, you must be willing to walk. Those at Rock Bottom are given a lesson in walking. If you listen, Rock Bottom teaches you that you should not sit at the foot of the mountain and pray to be carried to the top. You need to pray while you are climbing.

6. As you start to emerge from this awful place you become aware that you have been given a new beginning. Not a new beginning that erases the painful memories,

but a new beginning for a soul that has survived feelings more intense than anyone can ever know. This new beginning comes only to those brave and honest enough to keep the lessons of Rock Bottom secure in their memories.

When you leave Rock Bottom you will find yourself invited into a new community. This is the inspiring community of souls who have suffered and survived. Albert Schweitzer, you remember, called this "the fellowship of those who bear the mark of pain." This collection of individuals may be quite different from the community you were previously a part of. If you have learned from your experience, then Rock Bottom has changed you. If it doesn't kill you, this experience makes you stronger and wiser. This experience contains both of the fundamental qualities that produce growth. The descent into Rock Bottom is a humbling experience. The climb out of it is an *empowering* one. We maintain this growth to the extent that we keep the humility and empowerment alive within us.

There is a community of those who have suffered and survived. The bonds that are made here can be among the deepest, truest, and most honest that humans are capable of making.

One final note about Rock Bottom. I'm afraid anyone can fall into it. Just because you have decided to follow your yearning, survived dragons with honor, faced your shadow, and have learned how to learn, these will not make you immune to the worst kinds of suffering. If you are capable of doubt — which is the entrance to enlightenment — you are capable of falling into the despair that is Rock Bottom. Thus living with the capacity for doubt requires a certain amount of courage. This is, however, the same courage that will help you rise again should you fall.

Enlightenment and despair are not behind door number

one and door number two. They are behind the same door, and that door is doubt. No one is immune to despair. But we do have some control over what waits behind that door. Much depends on how we approach that door.

ENLIGHTENMENT

If life were a musical, this is the point where the really beautiful music would begin. It is here that one's soul emerges with the force and splendor of a sunrise. The lights go on and the pieces of life that were once hidden are now in full view. Feeling and thought flow into harmony, neither causing fear any longer. As the sun rises, it does not bring awesome power or complete certainty with it. More than anything, it brings peace. A well-earned peace.

The enlightened person is she who has learned to move in the face of doubt. She has approached this door with an acceptance that there will be times when life is confusing. She allows for the confusion and refuses to retreat when she runs into it. She has integrated her innocent child with her gallant warrior. She has harmonized her humility and her power. She can combat her confusion. She can play and dance with her doubt.

Enlightenment begins the final phase of the road to you. While it is possible to become enlightened and then lose it, this seldom occurs. Enlightenment is more of a permanent awakening. Once you look at life through enlightened eyes, it's hard to forget what you saw. The peace it brings carries an indelible stillness to your soul. Once you are enlightened, you are changed. In order to lose this, one would have to repress one's soul.

Enlightenment is a natural human experience. The word itself is not a part of everyone's language and thus many people have achieved enlightenment without calling it "enlighten-ment." What one calls this experience is, of course, not impor-tant. Remember, everyone has their own language. You use the description that best explains how you experience this passage.

Enlightenment can be explained in so many ways. But I believe it is composed of at least two events that can change people forever. One event affects the mind; the other affects the spirit. First, we become enlightened when we reduce the size of our ego. When this happens we can understand things as they are, rather than insisting that everything conform to what we think they should be. We can live with the fact that we might be wrong or that maybe we aren't as knowledgeable as we once hoped we were. A large ego blinds us. It makes us place de-mands on reality and when reality doesn't oblige, we end up distorting it. When we lighten our egos, we understand that the best teachers are the best students. An enlightened soul conducts an honest pursuit of knowledge. The enlightened teacher dances lightly and joyfully with the awareness that he may find out tomorrow that what he is teaching today is not completely correct. He doesn't carry the weight of having to control tomorrow.

A big ego can be more punishing than a guilty conscience. It distances you from those who might see your flaws. Intimacy then becomes more of a threat than a comfort. Like a ball and chain, it confines you to those arenas where you excel or where you are, at the very least, competent. If you're not good at it, you can't go there.

No one with a big ego can fly. They're just too heavy. They trudge. Image is everything in their weighted down world. Enthusiasm, excitement, and other forms of flight are, to put it mildly, controlled. Since they can't fly, they miss the perspec-tive one gets when lifted above ground zero.

When one's ego deflates, one feels the return of innocence. It's O.K. not to know. It's no problem to ask simple questions.

Image doesn't get in the way of the pursuit of intimacy or answers. You feel what you feel. You ask the questions that come to mind. On the psychological level, enlightenment means that you have become light enough to be real.

Second, on the spiritual plane, we become enlightened when we connect with the Light. The Light is the source of your calling, the force that called you and started you on the road to you. As I said in Chapter One, I cannot tell you what you will see when you connect with the Light. This is your experience, your lesson, your revelation. And what you see may grow clearer in time. It's not that the Light changes; it's just that your view and understanding may improve.

We are humbled and empowered by the Light. It confirms and affirms all that we have been through. The Light removes many of the petty doubts that tend to stick to us such as concerns about one's image (e.g., Am I tall enough? Am I smart enough?). Reaching the Light builds a quiet confidence. As this occurs, the doubts about whether or not you can fulfill your calling start to lose their volume. The doubt turns into determination and conviction. Because one is now psychologically lighter (and no longer must carry a heavy ego), more energy is available to apply to one's work and relationships.

When you first felt your yearning, you became aware that you have a meaning and a mission in your life. Now you are aware of its importance. When you encounter the Light, you may actually begin to hear that beautiful music begin to play. Your pieces are coming together. They are coming together to fulfill a calling. You realize that you are meant to be the person who is capable of acting on your calling, be that a parent, a teacher, a builder, an artist, or any combination of paths. Included in everyone's calling is the urge to be a decent human being. Contact with the Light provides an increased strength that assists you to become all that you are called to be. It does not protect you from failure, pain or suffering. It helps you build the strength to stay on (and sometimes return to) course.

Many people call the Light "God." When they connect with God they feel the strength that comes from knowing what God wants them to do. They also emerge with a stronger spirituality because they have felt the presence of God. They are no longer limited by other people's stories of Who or What God is. They begin to see for themselves.

No one is an expert on God. It seems that God wants us to have some doubt so that we always have room to grow. So the stories we are told about God are, like ourselves, imperfect. No one really meets God through a story. We, instead, come to know God through experience. We will not experience God until we are willing to recognize Him and stand in His presence.

There are those who fall into spiritual crises when they reach the Light, because It does not resemble the God they had prepared themselves for. Their stories don't match what they see. In this situation, some go back and look for new teachers. Others question if what they are experiencing is real. They may spend years motionless (or restless) at this point trying to decide how to interpret what they are experiencing.

A big ego can deny the reality of God if it threatens one's self-image. I'm afraid this is common in our day and age. There are many people on the verge of believing but who just can't touch the Light. Instead of talking about God, they talk about "my Higher Power." I think most of these people feel the presence of God; they just don't want to accept it. One man told me his music was his higher power. And several people have told me that the Alcoholics Anonymous group was their higher power. Others have told me it was nature. I've even treated a few clients who insisted their higher power was Satan.

It seems, though, that without exception each of these individuals communicated the unspoken message: I don't want to believe in God. All of these people were wounded by the dragons in their lives. Somehow they came to the conclusion that these difficult creatures were sent by God to torment them. Then, in time, they reached the point where they could no longer avoid recognizing God's presence. Denial can only go so far. So they accept the higher power, but change it so that it is not God. For some, this psycho-spiritual compromise can last for years. They live on the verge of God.

Enlightenment comes only to those willing to look honestly at the Light. Like every point along the way on the road to you, the journey can end here. You can turn away from the Light. In spite of all you've done to get here, you can turn away.

On the psychological level, enlightenment means lightening the ego and becoming more willing to accept the world as it is. On the spiritual level it means connecting with the Light, the force that began this journey by accepting your calling. Psychological enlightenment precedes spiritual enlightenment. It's the humility that leads to empowerment.

Enlightenment is a transition. You are changed forever. When you reach the Light, you arrive at a place that never leaves you. The experience is too powerful. It is an overwhelmingly positive trauma. There is no leaving it behind. When you find the source of your calling, you begin a new phase of life. The searching is now over. Now it no longer makes sense to conceptualize life as a journey. When you find your Sun, your roots grow strong and ground you to a place where you feel that Sun. You continue to learn but it's not enough to learn; you must also teach. You will continue to grow but it is not enough to grow; you must promote growth in others.

Enlightenment is a destination. It begins with brief yet powerful moments of insight. These are the candles that lead you to a beautiful Light. The Light shows you the person you are meant to be. This person is a product of what the Light has called you to be and the experiences that you have encountered while you have journeyed. If you decide to look back, you will find that these experiences, as difficult as some have been, have prepared you well for the final phase of becoming the person you are meant to be. Your journey will provide a lifetime of lessons when it is reexamined with an enlightened mind and spirit.

One of the most intriguing aspects about enlightenment is that as powerful as it is, it is equally subtle. Enlightened people have little need to dwell on their enlightenment. Most enlightened people never even consider using the word enlightenment; it's not in their language. Then there's the paradox that's described in the Hindu proverb: "Anyone who thinks he is enlightened certainly is not!"

In this sense, enlightenment is like virtue. Those who possess virtue tend not to feel like they do. It's hard to find a courageous person who will describe herself as courageous. The same holds true for those who display kindness, humility, generosity, patience, etc. Besides, enlightened people have more important things to do than bask in what they have accomplished. They're not baskers. They're more aware of their ignorance than they are of their enlightenment. They are aware of the Light but perhaps not the enlightenment.

Enlightenment is a destination. We travel toward it. While the Light can make Itself known to anyone at any time, people most often connect with It by making a deliberate, honest, and courageous attempt to follow their callings. The yearning is the Light calling us to move toward It. There is, however, one important exception to this. As I said, the Light can appear to us at any time. It can appear to those who have turned completely away from It. It may also appear to one who has never lifted a finger to answer the yearning. The Light appears to urge that person to move toward It. The Light can pursue us at any time. But there is, I think, one particular point in life when we are likely to feel the Light journey toward us. At this point we seem more willing to open ourselves to the Light. This willingness comes at the time of our death.

I believe that it is a common human phenomenon that we have a sense of our death as the time draws near. This may not be at a conscious level but it is real nonetheless. This is not a fear of death but, rather, an awareness of it. There is an enlightenment that can come in our final days. This is why people are so often remembered for what we share in the final chapters of our lives. It is here where we may teach our most important lessons. It is here that we are capable of achieving our closest relationship with God. Consequently, it may be at this point when we become most enlightened.

It is also here that we are most willing to accept our innocence. Just as we started our lives with a magnificent innocence, we have the opportunity to take this innocence to new heights at the other end of our lives. Innocence is crucial. It frees people to learn but, just as importantly, it frees us to love. The innocence that grows through enlightenment enhances our ability to learn and love. Enlightened people, like small children, live a life of learning. Every leaf teaches. Everyone they meet carries a lesson or two. Innocence maximizes the power of their encounter with the Light. Through their innocence they devote themselves to loving and learning from the Light.

We can become enlightened gradually or suddenly. When enlightenment comes suddenly one may hit a crisis of significant proportions. Much will depend on how well the stories one has been told about God and life match one's direct experience. Those who have been taught by enlightened teachers usually have an easier time when they themselves become enlightened. These fortunate souls have been prepared well for their encounter with God. Not everyone, however, is as fortunate. There are those who have learned stories that make it hard to accept the existence and the lessons of the Light.

The Light can correct bad teaching if you allow It to teach you. This requires what is sometimes referred to as a leap of faith. You may be asked to free yourself from your stories. You may be encouraged to disregard stories that are fundamental to your identity. When you encounter the Light, your identity changes — maybe a little, maybe a lot. Even if the stories you have been told about the Light (or what I call God) match perfectly with what you experience when you encounter It, you are still changed. For even in this case, you are changed in that you have taken ownership of your stories. Your story of God is no longer someone else's story that has been handed down to you. You now have your own story and your own relationship with God.

For some, experiencing the Light is so different from the stories they've been living that, when they do begin their own relationship with God, they describe themselves as being born again. For many, this is an accurate description. The change can be that profound.

Enlightenment, you see, is about more than gaining wisdom. It's also about finding inspiration. The Light does not give out lottery numbers. It doesn't pick heads or tails, nor does It serve as a cosmic computer that spews forth cold facts. The wisdom you receive from the Light is the kind that moves you. The Light provides you with knowledge that inspires you. As you get closer to the Light, the energy builds. Inspiration may turn to conviction and passion (forms of love). Those who accept the Light into their lives become wiser, more energetic, and more loving.

And so it might seem that with this increased power, people might want to use it all in pursuit of that great human temptation — control. But such is not the case. Before approaching the Light, one must shed one's oversized ego and abandon the race to control the world. Then the Light Itself carries the message that you can only love the things that you will not control. The enlightened person lets God be God and not only what he wants Him to be. The enlightened person does not dominate her world. She loves it. The enlightened person does not seek control. She seeks love and wisdom. She builds her relationship with God. As she reaches and connects with the Light, "*My* will be done" turns into "*Thy* will be done." Control is replaced by love. Cold is replaced by warm.

Enlightenment, with all it can do to empower you, also humbles. Though you may float for a time, it ultimately leaves you more grounded. Humility may be the final phase of enlightenment. All truly enlightened people come to the realization that even though they have embraced the Light, they still must mow the lawn, brush their teeth, vacuum the carpet, and eat lunch. There is a Zen teaching that says, "After enlightenment, the laundry." After empowerment, humility. After humility, empowerment.

CONCLUSION

Enlightenment is a destination. It begins with the revelation that your journey is over. Your mission in life may be just starting, but your journey is completed. You have found your place. You belong where you can see the Light.

At this point on the road to you, traveling will not bring you closer to God or make you more effective in doing His work. Enlightened souls are both learners and teachers. They have the innocence to move lightly with ignorance and strongly with conviction. Doubt is no longer intimidating but understood as a door to a new lesson. They may lose their keys more than ever or bungle the punch line on all their jokes, but they live with the awareness that they are standing in the presence of God. They have lost their ego and found the Light.

Finally, even though enlightenment is the beginning of an arrival, it may bring losses with it. People who may have been dear to you may not understand your changes. Because your eyes are ready to see It, does not mean everyone else's are. Because connecting with the Light can put all your previous experiences in a new perspective, your arrival may signal a significant change in you. Through your awakening, you may have to say good-bye to the person you thought you were. This may mean giving up your bow-ties or your protective coating of sarcasm and cynicism. You may have to atone for sins you didn't know you were committing. You may have to apologize for who you were.

Enlightenment is one of the most important achievements in life. Here you learn that you are standing in the presence of God. It is also here that you learn that, in spite of all you have survived and accomplished, you are no better than anyone else.

"After enlightenment, the laundry."

CHAPTER EIGHT

THE ARRIVAL

The person you are meant to be is the person who can live your calling. The road to you leads you to the place you find faith in what you are called to do. Here you become the person that only you can be.

Moving into your mission, you come to feel a power that you've never known. You've survived adversity with your honor intact; you've faced your dark side; you've humbled yourself and you've empowered yourself. You've faced the Light and allowed It to move you. And in the process, you've learned that the Light that humbles you is the same Light that empowers you. When you honestly accept the humility, you find the power.

Earlier I quoted an anonymous sage as saying, "Leap and the net will appear." When you leap toward the Light, something more striking occurs. In this case we can say, "Leap and your wings will appear." The paradox is that when you grow your wings, you become more grounded. You lose the desire to fly away. Instead you develop a focus on what matters most. With this focus comes stability. What matters most to you is precisely what you are called to serve. You are now ready to serve in a powerfully spiritual way.

The road to you leads you to find how you will serve life. You may be asked to make a variety of contributions or you may be led to a singular form of service. In any case, as you reach your destination on your path to self discovery, you are willing and able to identify your mission and say out loud, "This is what I am here to do!"

When you arrive at this destination you will have balance in your life. There will be a balance to your awareness. You are now aware of what goes on inside you, the thoughts and feelings. You are equally aware of what surrounds you. You have developed an awareness of people and nature. You are balanced. You are aware of God's voice that speaks within you as well as His messages that come from beyond.

Balance accounts for much of the personal stability that comes with your arrival. Here one can balance doubt and confidence, patience and aggressiveness, thinking and feeling, nurturing and the need to be nurtured, generosity and self-care, strength and weakness, joy and sorrow. When you follow your calling you develop balance in your life. You, though far from flawless, develop a stability that enhances your competence.

It might seem that this stability would build self-esteem. Well, yes and no. When someone immerses herself in her life's work, she rarely even considers her self-esteem. At this level of development people tend not to dwell on self-judgment. It's a distraction that usually has little benefit. They are quite capable of feeling good about what they do. This satisfaction can help motivate their efforts. So, in this sense, yes, they do have high self-esteem. It's just that this is not the sort of thing people at this level of development care much about.

What do they care about? They care about the life they are called to. A man who is called to be a husband and a father cares about his family. Once he finds his mission, he settles. He does not stop growing; he settles into the life he is called to. He grows by learning about how children grow and about communicating with his wife. He grows by learning more about himself as a husband and a father.

A calling does not lead you to a job in the sense of a butcher, baker, or candlestick maker. A calling pulls you to a way of living. And while everyone's mission is unique, there are qualities that are a part of everyone's callings. We are all called to be decent human beings. As such, we are all called to recognize the rights of others. We are called to improve the world. Each of us is urged to take as much of the world as we can and make it better. A decent human being works to improve the quality of life for all living things. She does what she can to support justice. She lives her life as an example of decency.

A decent human being makes decency a goal in life. He realizes that this doesn't happen by accident and thus works to improve the quality of his own character. Although this character can grow deeper and wiser, it is not likely to change to an indecent style of life. This soul has come too far to; priorities are too clear. As decency grows and becomes more apparent, this person may find himself in a position of leadership. He becomes an attractive leader for several reasons. First, he is a powerful role model. Second, people realize his honesty and feel he can be trusted. And third, because people can sense his virtue, they can count on him to make ethical and moral decisions. His stability lends stability to any group he leads.

When someone has arrived, they balance stability and growth. They become better at their mission. Beyond this self-improvement, they allow their callings to evolve. One mission may serve as the foundation or launching pad for another. A woman who has spent thirty years raising children may feel the pull to move on to something else once her last child leaves home. Someone who has worked most of his life in a particular career may, at some point, retire from that vocation. What is important to realize, however, is that when this mother's last child leaves home or when this man retires, the person they are meant to be does not change. It merely moves into a new mission.

You are not really called to a job such as a carpenter or a parent. You are called to a life. Granted, a large portion of this life may involve a career, but there is more. We are all called to be decent human beings. We are all called to learn from our life experiences and then use what we've learned in the service of decency.

In my spare time I teach in the graduate programs at several of the universities in the St. Louis area. Specifically, I teach master's and doctoral level courses in counseling. On occasion I teach the entry level course in the master's program. This is the first course for students who've decided to pursue a graduate degree in counseling.

It's not uncommon for one-third or more of these students to be middle-aged or older. These folks have already raised their children or, in some cases, retired from the job they called their "career." Usually these students are quite nervous. You can almost hear the critical voices in their heads saying, "You're too old for this! You're just being foolish! It's too late to change!" Hearing all this silent racket, I make this Lesson Number One: "This is not a course for beginners," I tell them. "It just happens to be the first course in this program. This class, if we are to accomplish anything worthwhile, must build upon all the life experiences you bring with you to this classroom. Again, this is not a course for beginners. This is a course for those who are willing to learn from experience. This is a class for those who have already learned a great deal."

While I'm saying this, many of the younger adult students are fumbling with their pens and pads preparing to write down the first assignment. These students worry me. They only know about learning from books. The older students (some so scared that they've already read the texts before the first class) always appear grateful. They don't want to throw away all that they've learned in their lives. Nor should they.

What looks like a change in you may well be the evolution of you. When someone encounters the Light, she comes to understand that she has been called to a special life. She begins to find and feel balance as she touches a growing conviction to live the life of a decent human being. From this point forward there will be a stability in her life. Certainly there will be times of sorrow, confusion, and failure, but these events are not likely to remove her from the person she is meant to be.

Her center, her stabilizing force, is no longer her ego or her shadow. Nor is she ruled by her dragons. She finds stability in the Light. One way the Light teaches is through experience. The mother who becomes a gardener who then becomes a teacher may be true to her calling throughout each new experience. In each arena she may well be the person she is meant to be. She remains true to herself and God as her calling evolves. As she grows, certain fundamental qualities remain constant. In the rocker, in the soil, and in the classroom she remains a decent human being devoted to the mission she has been given.

The human ego is inherently unstable. It is not the entity to build an identity upon. It inflates and deflates at a moment's notice. The ego leads you into captivity. It follows the expectations and approval of others. Even during those times when you have reduced the size of your ego to the point where it no longer runs your life, your accomplishment will be only temporary if you do not replace it with something. If you do not replace your ego with something healthier, it will eventually resume its place as the center of your being.

The road to you leads to an understanding that you answer to a higher authority than even the largest ego. When you reach the source of your calling you find the force that — if you accept It — can lead you in a way that your ego cannot. When you reach the Light your focus moves outward. Here people lose their interest in the question, "Who am I?" and become more concerned with: "What am I to do?" "*My* will be done" grows into "*Thy* will be done."

You may not need to name the source of your calling. But many of us do. I believe the source to be God and I believe that we come to see God as the Light at the end of a journey. You see, the road to you is the road to your spirituality. Your spiritual self is your one true and constant self. It grows while it remains stable. It blossoms while it maintains stillness. It allows for a wide variety of feelings, experiences, beliefs, and questions, and it is capable of preserving balance in beings as complex as ourselves.

You are meant to be the person who can fulfill your calling. The qualities you need to develop are the qualities you will need to answer your calling. Certain qualities seem to be needed to live just about all callings. These characteristics might include determination, a certain amount of confidence, a sense of humor, courage, patience, honesty, and a work ethic. Then there are qualities that are unique to your special mission. A parent, for instance, needs to learn how to express love, and develop a willingness to hold on and to let go. A good parent also needs to develop leadership abilities. A writer must be one who continually seeks knowledge. She must be honest and humble and willing to be led by her creativity.

The person you are meant to be is the person who can fulfill your calling. Besides the personality characteristics just mentioned, you have to keep yourself physically fit enough to do what you are asked to do. This means taking care of your physical health. You need to exercise what control you have over your body's well-being. Fitness is not selfish. Your body can empower you. Physical energy can be a great aid in your efforts to live the life that is right for you. Sooner or later, your body will also humble you. If you let it, your body will teach you about both power and humility.

If you do not accept your limitations, you will be lost and confused when you push yourself to your limits. There will be times when this kind of extraordinary effort will be necessary and it should lead to pride rather than confusion. There will always be limits to your power but there will also be power in your limits. When you touch them you will have gone as far as you can in that moment. Many people never get that far in their entire lives.

As power and humility grow in you, you will become grounded in life and the spirit that runs through all of life. You may then come to realize that your contributions are for all time. You may learn that you are leaving your legacy for all that follow you. This legacy may include life-saving discoveries or leadership that changes the course of history. But, more than anything, please keep in mind that the greatest legacy you can ever leave is your decency. People are rarely remembered for anything else.

A human being's decency ripples forever through the generations. It passes through those who are touched by it eventually creating an energy that survives the death of its source. One's earthly name may not be attached to this decency for more than a generation or two. But this matters little. The name was never important. It was the force. All that was put in motion by decency. Once born, the decency lives forever.

Decency is a stable force. It lends stability to those who carry it. It doesn't bring perfection. But the attitude it brings never demands perfection. The focus isn't on perfection because your focus is no longer on yourself. Your focus is on how to make ours a more decent world.

You learn that your life does not belong to you; it never did. You are part of a larger scheme. Your part is to contribute. If you do not, there will be a void, a wound in the heart of the universe that will last forever. No one else can provide what you refuse to contribute.

The road to you leads you to the place where you make your contributions. These contributions, in their own way, last forever. On a psychological level your destination is the development of balance in your life. Although the scale may swing from time to time, it is balanced in your understanding of yourself and your confidence that you can transcend the obstacles that stand between you and the life you have been called to. On the spiritual level, your journey has brought you to the Light, the source of your calling. The lessons of the Light are endless and everyone receives his or her own special direction. But there is a lesson that seems to be given to everyone who encounters the Light. Your life is much larger and more significant than you knew. You are here to make a contribution. The fact that you are alive means you have something important to give.

Upon reaching your destination on the road to you, you discover what you may have suspected all along. You are meant to be a decent human being. If you cannot accept this, it is probably because you have too many fears of inadequacy lurking in your shadow which must be dealt with before you can accept your destination and the call to decency.

Decency is a self-perpetuating force. Once you really feel it and really live it, it tends to stay with you. Each act of decency strengthens your relationship with the Light. Living in what can be a selfish world does not squelch the positive feeling that comes to you when you live decency. There is a rightness to it. You may contribute to the world in many ways. But your real legacy will be your decency.

REFERENCES

Chapter One

1. Rohr, R. *Quest for the Grail*. New York: Crossroad, 1994, p. 109.
2. Pearson, C.S., *Awakening the Heroes Within*. San Francisco: Harper Collins, 1991.

Chapter Two

1. Landman, J., *Regret*. Oxford University Press, 1993.
2. White, W.L. & Wall, P., *The Call to Write*. Lighthouse Institute Publishing, 1995.
3. Pearson, C.S., *The Hero Within*. San Francisco: Harper, 1989.

Chapter Three

1. Clarke, J.R., *The Importance of Being Imperfect*. New York: David McKay Company, Inc., 1961.

Chapter Four

1. Daniels, M. *Self-Discovery the Jungian Way*. New York: Routledge, 1992.
2. Ibid., p. 45.
3. Whitmont, E.C., "The Evolution of the Shadow" in Zweig, C. & Abrams, J. (Eds.), *Meeting the Shadow*, New York: G.P. Putnam's Sons, 1991, p. 17.
4. Miller, W.A., "Finding the Shadow in Daily Life" in Zweig, C. & Abrams, J. (Eds.), *Meeting the Shadow*, New York: G.P. Putnam's Sons, 1991, p. 40.
5. Bly, R., "The Long Bag We Drag Behind Us" in Zweig, C. & Abrams, J. (Eds.), *Meeting the Shadow*, New York: G.P. Putnam's Sons, 1991, p. 6.

6. Zweig, C. & Abrams, J., *Meeting the Shadow: The Hidden Power of the Dark Side of Human Nature.* New York: G.P. Putnam's Sons, 1991.

Chapter Six

1. Kabal-Zinn, J., *Wherever You Go, There You Are.* New York: Hyperion, 1994, p. xv.

Robert J. Furey, PhD is a psychotherapist in private practice in St. Louis, Missouri. He has taught in the graduate programs at several universities and is the author of *So I'm Not Perfect, Facing Fear, The Joy of Kindness,* and *Called By Name.* Dr. Furey lives in St. Louis County with his wife and five children.

To find out more about his workshops, contact:

> Robert J. Furey, PhD
> c/o ALBA HOUSE
> 2187 Victory Blvd.
> Staten Island, NY 10314-6603